MEN AND SUBSTANCE ABUSE

MEN AND

SUBSTANCE ABUSE

Narratives of
Addiction and Recovery

Judith Grant

FIRST**FORUM**PRESS

A DIVISION OF LYNNE RIENNER PUBLISHERS, INC. • BOULDER & LONDON

Published in the United States of America in 2012 by
FirstForumPress
A division of Lynne Rienner Publishers, Inc.
1800 30th Street, Boulder, Colorado 80301
www.firstforumpress.com

and in the United Kingdom by
FirstForumPress
A division of Lynne Rienner Publishers, Inc.
3 Henrietta Street, Covent Garden, London WC2E 8LU

Library of Congress Cataloging-in-Publication Data
Grant, Judith, 1942–
Men and substance abuse: narratives of addiction and recovery / Judith Grant.
  Includes bibliographical references and index.
ISBN 978-1-935049-48-7 (hc: alk. paper)
  1. Drug addicts—United States. 2. Men—Substance use—United States.
3. Alcoholics—United States. 4. Drug addicts—Rehabilitation—United States.
5. Alcoholics—Rehabilitation—United States. I. Title.
HV5825.G693 2012
616.8600811—dc23   2011052463

British Cataloguing in Publication Data
A Cataloguing in Publication record for this book
is available from the British Library.

This book was produced from digital files prepared
using the FirstForumComposer.

Printed and bound in the United States of America

The paper used in this publication meets the requirements
of the American National Standard for Permanence of
Paper for Printed Library Materials Z39.48-1992.

5 4 3 2 1

Contents

Tables

Acknowledgments

Many individuals helped in the creation of this book. The book would not have been possible without the assistance of the men I interviewed, and I thank them for sharing with me their addiction and recovery experiences. Their answers to my many questions were testaments to their courage and creativity in escaping addiction. My hope is that their documented voices will encourage other men as they struggle to enter recovery. As Bobo, one of my participants, expressed it: "I can say that I appreciate this, I hope you end up publishin' a book. I hope . . . that this gets in there and somebody actually reads it, and maybe a light bulb will go off in their head." I hope I have done justice to all the men's stories.

I also want to thank those special students of mine who transcribed and coded my interviews in preparation for the analysis: Michael Perkins, Joanne Lucier, Jennifer Foden, and Carleigh Taggart, all outstanding honor students. Thank you, too, to Renee Snellings, another exceptional student, who worked so tirelessly on the final analysis, and to David Bird, who was relentless in his final edit of the book. They were a delightful group of students to work with, and they provided immeasurable help toward the writing of the book.

I also want to thank Andrew Berzanskis for his editorial expertise throughout this project and Rick Huard for finalizing the index and typesetting the book for me. Finally, I thank my husband, Adrian, who has been my advisor and critic throughout my research work and has consistently encouraged me to get my thoughts down on paper in order to tell the men's stories.

1

Men and Substance Abuse

I think if I had something to say to anybody ... was gonna read this
stuff is, that if you really want a different life you can have it, you can
have a whole different life. You gotta want it more than anything. And
it's worth it, that's the thing, no matter how bad in the beginning ...
it's gonna feel and it will feel very, very bad, 'cause it's worth it.
(Duane)

This book recounts the experiences of 25 men who have been abstaining
from the use of drugs and/or alcohol for 18 months or more in the Ozark
region of the United States. Based on qualitative interviews, this book
examines the processes of addiction to and recovery from such
substances for participants. Using the paradigm of symbolic interaction,
this book considers how participants make meaning of activities, actions
and interactions with themselves and others as they process addiction
and recovery changes. Participants interviewed for this study are the
experts in their lives and relevant data are generated from their stories of
addiction and recovery processes. As Duane states in the above quote,
perhaps the men's stories will encourage others who are addicted to
substances to "have a whole different life," as they consider their
addiction and recovery processes, thus affirming the stories documented
in this book.

The theoretical perspective of this study is grounded in symbolic
interaction and individual self and social identity theory as indicated
within the social act (Mead 1934/1938). In this book, I am concerned
with how men's individual selves and social identities change in relation
to addiction and recovery processes. My approach is to make sense of
participants' experiences by asking what they are like, what in their
thinking and feelings underlies their behavior, how they come to be as
they are (i.e., in addiction and in their recovery), and what pressures
they receive from their social environments.

For participants in this study addiction implies that the ingestion of
controlled substances: (1) causes problems in their lives by interfering

with daily living, and (2) participants lose the ability to predict their loss of control (McMurran 1994). In this study, each participant self-identifies himself as a man formerly addicted to controlled substances and now abstinent in his recovery. Although, generally, alcohol is not considered an illegal substance within the literature (Adrian, Lundy and Eliany 1996; Denzin 1987a), it is often qualified as a drug that causes many individual and social problems within people's lives (Goode 1999; Adrian et al. 1996; Blackwell, Thurston and Graham 1996; Currie 1993). It is a substance that many of these participants identify as the one they abuse to a great extent, and the substance from which they must recover through various means.

I highlight in this study then an understanding of how these men shape their behaviors in their processes of addiction and recovery. I agree with Stevens, Berto, Frick, McSweeney, Schaaf, Tartari, Turnbull, Trinkl, Uchtenhagen, Waidner and Werdenich (2007) that a critical approach to an understanding of drug users would be to amplify their voices as they narrate their experiences. Whiteacre (n.d., p. 21) further argues that "drawing out the voices of drug users suggests looking for ways to allow them to tell their own stories. Such an approach provides a discourse of drug users' own reality rather than researchers' images of drug users." And, too, as Denzin and Lincoln (2008, p. 46) argue, "Telling the stories of marginalized people can help to create a public space requiring others to hear what they do not want to hear." Further, Beverley (2000, p. 556) states that

> The voice that speaks to the reader through the text … [takes] the form of an *I* that demands to be recognized, that wants or needs to stake a claim to our attention.

The purpose of this study is twofold: (1) to describe, from participants' perspectives, how they became addicted to drugs and/or alcohol and how they discontinued their use of such substances through their recovery processes, and (2) to analyze the methods that enabled these participants to become addicted as well as to recover from their addictions. Here I argue that recovery is the regaining of something lost or taken away; it is a developmental process that is dynamic, fluid and can enhance growth (Prochaska, DiClemente and Norcross 1992). Such a developmental process is highlighted throughout this study as participants "told" their stories of their specific experiences.

Knowledge about gender differences in pathways into addiction and recovery has established that women and men differ in their use/abuse of substances (Haseltine 2000; Abbot 1995; Van Den Bergh 1991). The following section reviews such differences.

The Problem and Significance of Men's Addiction

In studies on men and alcohol, men report higher levels of consumption of alcohol and report more frequent use of alcohol than women (Grant, Harford, Dawson, Chou, Dufour and Pickering 1994; Grella and Joshi 1999; Hser, Huang, Teruya and Anglin 2003; Liebschutz, Savetsky, Saitz, Horton, Lloyd-Travaglini and Samet 2002; Majer, Jason, Ferrari and North 2002; Olenick and Chalmers 1991; Peters, Strozier, Murrin and Kearns 1997; Pirard, Sharon, Kang, Angarita and Gastfriend 2005; Reiger, Farmer, Rae, Locke, Keith, Judd and Goodwin 1990). For example, the Epidemiologic Catchment Area Study, a large survey study conducted in the early 1980s with a representative sample from throughout the United States, showed a number of interesting differences between men and women. For prevalence rates of alcohol use disorders, men were more than five times as likely to have an alcohol-use disorder (Reiger et al. 1990).

Some more recent statistics are provided from the Longitudinal Alcohol Epidemiologic Survey related to the prevalence of alcohol dependence and abuse diagnosis in men and women. When only alcohol dependence was considered, the prevalence rates were 2.1 percent for men and 1.2 percent for women. However, when both alcohol abuse and dependence were considered the gender differences widened. Men were three times more likely to have a diagnosis of alcohol abuse or dependence than were women (Grant et al. 1994).

Men also report different reasons for using alcohol than women. Specifically, they tend to use alcohol in social gatherings, to help them be more congenial, and to use it in a gregarious fashion (Olenick and Chalmers 1991). In addition, men are more likely than women to perceive their drinking as a source of difficulties in their lives (i.e., legal, financial, family, and work-related) (Schober and Annis 1996).

Numerous studies suggest that excessive alcohol consumption and alcohol abuse are significant risk factors for marital violence (Fagan, Stewart and Hasen 1983; Leonard, Bromet, Parkinson, Day and Ryan 1985; Leonard and Blane 1992). For example, Leonard et al. (1985) reported a relationship between physical marital conflict and a diagnosis of alcohol abuse or alcohol dependency in a group of male factory workers.

Drug dependent men use drugs in order to socialize, to get "high" and as an adventure (Haseltine 2000). They are more likely to be drug injectors than women and more likely to support their addiction by drug dealing or theft (Powis, Griffiths, Gossop and Strang 1996). In a study of cocaine-using men, Bierut, Strickland, Thompson, Afful and Cottler (2008) found that in addition to cocaine use, the use of nicotine, alcohol, marijuana and other illicit drug use was the norm with these men. This indicates that some cocaine-using men may engage in multiple substance use or polysubstance use.

In a study of gay men and alcohol and drugs by Irwin and Morgenstern (2005), a high proportion of participants met the diagnostic criteria for both drug- and alcohol-use disorders. A surprisingly high proportion of participants also met diagnostic criteria for drug abuse and dependence. Irwin and Morgenstern (2005) suggest concurrent alcohol and drug use to be higher among gay men than the general population, after comparing their findings to the National Drug and Alcoholism Unit Survey. The National Drug and Alcoholism Treatment Unit Survey indicates that about 40 percent of those who receive substance-abuse treatment have disorders related to both alcohol and drug abuse. In this study, roughly 60 percent of the men met DSM-IV criteria for both drug- and alcohol-use disorders (Irwin and Morgenstern 2005, p. 132).

Studies that have concentrated on the intimate environment of family influences, poor parenting; parental absence, separation, or divorce; family conflict; or deviant behavior among family members have found that excessive use of alcohol and/or drugs on the part of the parents influences male children in experimenting with and continuing addictive behaviors (Baer and Corrado 1974; Chassin, Curran, Hussong and Colder 1996; Nurco, Kinlock, O'Grady and Hanlon 1998). For example, Nurco et al. (1998) found in a sample of 601 males that disruption in family structure (i.e., parental divorce or separation) prior to age 11 was significantly associated with narcotic addiction.

Other studies consider high rates of childhood physical and sexual victimization among alcohol and/or drug-dependent men (Blood and Cornwall 1996; Chassin et al. 1996; Clark, Masson, Delucchi, Hall and Sees 2001; Fiorentine, Pilati and Hillhouse 1999; Gil-Rivas, Fiorentine, Anglin and Taylor 1997; Liebschutz et al. 2002; Pirard et al. 2005). Blood and Cornwall (1996) found that 62 percent of men who reported sexual abuse also reported physical abuse, compared to 32 percent of those who reported no sexual abuse. They also found that sexually abused adolescents reported an earlier onset of alcohol and other drug use than did nonabused adolescents.

In addition, extant research suggests that a strong predictor of adolescent drug use is the extent to which one associates with other adolescents who use drugs (Bahr, Marcos and Maughan 1995; Elliott,

Huizinga and Ageton 1985). McIntosh and McKeganey's (2002) findings suggest the main reasons for participants' initial drug use were curiosity and a desire to comply with the expectations of others, especially peers.

Interestingly, Bahr et al. (1995) found that familial contributions were not found to directly influence alcohol and/or drug use in youths, but instead were found to be the onset to association with deviant, drug-using peers. They found that the influence of family bonds operates primarily through peer association. Lower family bonds and drug or alcohol abusing family members increased the likelihood of an adolescent associating with peers who drink or use drugs. Similarly, Nurco et al. (1998) found that children with deviant parents and those who lack a close relationship with nondeviant parents were more likely than other children to associate with deviant peers and to be vulnerable to peers' influences.

In addition to peer influence, studies have found an individual's community/neighborhood to be influential for drug use (Bierut et al. 2008). Bierut et al. (2008) found that when comparing cocaine dependent males and their siblings to individuals from their same neighborhood and siblings, rates of drug use were elevated in the community-based comparison group compared to population-based samples/studies. Community-based comparison groups were matched by zip codes suggesting that neighborhood factors contributed to these elevated rates of drug use and dependence.

In addition to looking at the addicts' initiation into alcohol and drug use, McIntosh and McKeganey (2002) examined the progression into abuse and dependence. In terms of the succession to regular use, participants offered a combination of explanations/factors influencing this transition. These included an unconscious "drift" rather than as a result of a deliberate decision; the influence of relationships or peer groups who provided opportunity and encouragement to use more regularly; boredom resulting from unemployment or poor recreational activities; to cope with life problems and escape from reality; or to overcome feelings of personal inadequacy, such as shyness or lack of confidence. In contrast, participants' escalating use was driven by a continuing desire to experiment and find new "highs," as well as the need to satisfy ever rising tolerance thresholds (McIntosh and McKeganey 2002).

According to McIntosh and McKeganey (2002), recognition by individuals that they were addicted could take anything from a few weeks to several months, depending on the drug being used and the addict's ability to support his/her habit. For most of the interviewees, recognition usually came with the experience of withdrawal symptoms and the realization that they needed drugs to function normally, which often came when they were deprived of them for some reason, such as a lack of money. Occasionally, family/friends would inform addicts that they thought they had a problem, although this was less common than one might expect. It is also clear from this study that once addicts became dependent their lives became dominated by the necessity to feed their habit, with the need to obtain money becoming their overriding preoccupation. Often this led to lives involving manipulation and deception of others, along with engaging in crimes such as theft/shoplifting. Many of the participants also ended up spending a period in prison and experiencing deterioration in health as a consequence of their use.

In terms of recovery, as individuals increasingly experience difficulties in a variety of areas of life function, they begin to contemplate the need to change their use patterns and to initiate a process of self-change (Marlatt, Baer, Donovan and Kivlahan 1988). Ebaugh (1988, p. 1) defines this process of change as a role exit; "the process of disengagement from a role that is central to one's self-identity and the reestablishment of an identity in a new role that takes into account one's ex-role." Ebaugh (1988) suggests four stages, including first doubts (begin to question and experience doubts about one's role commitment), seeking alternatives (an evaluation of the costs and benefits associated with an alternative role), turning points (events that force one to consider doing something different), and creating the ex-role (emotionally removing one's self from a previous role while experiencing social expectations based on a new one).

Anderson and Bondi (1998) explore race and gender variations in the processes of exiting a drug-addict role. Similar to Ebaugh (1988), they found their participants' role exit began with a doubt period. For the Black males in their study, their doubting period was characterized by questioning their drug use as blocking their opportunities for personal growth and narrowing their life options. On the other hand, White males reported that a burnout from the drug-role occurred which included a frustration with complications surrounding their drug use. They were not achieving euphoria from the drugs that they once felt and they were experiencing serious financial debt.

There is considerable agreement among researchers that the actual shift from the drug-addict role begins with a "turning point" (Biernacki 1986; Brown 1985; Ebaugh 1988). Normally these "points" are characterized by an event that serves as the end to one role and the beginning of a new one (Anderson and Bondi 1998). Such "turning points" are an essential step on the road to recovery from addiction (Ebaugh 1988).

Ebaugh (1988) notes four specific types of "turning points': specific events, last straws, time-related factors, and either/or alternatives. Anderson and Bondi (1998) found that for both Black and White males their turning points pertained to either/or alternatives following an arrest or drug treatment to shorten a prison stay. Other turning points were reported such as concern for job decline or termination, financial loss, health-related decline and significant others, more often by White males.

McIntosh and McKeganey (2002) identify some more common reasons given by addicts which promote their process of recovery. In particular, burnout is reported to be one of the most frequent precursors to recovery, as it seems that sustaining a habit can become an exceptionally difficult and demanding task associated with many problems. This is demonstrated in numerous studies, like that of Frykholm (1985) and Simpson, Joe, Lehman and Sells (1986), where addicts' main reason for stopping was that they were "tired of the life" or words to that effect.

Several studies have also shown that the influence of significant others, such as partners or children can be important in the decision to quit (Frykholm 1985; Simpson et al.1986; Smart 1994; Waldorf 1983). For example, Simpson et al. (1986) report that more than half of their sample stated "family responsibilities" were important in their decision to stop, while about a third cited pressure from family members was important.

Another important factor reported to be influential in the decision to stop is deteriorating health or the fear of health problems (Simpson et al. 1986; Waldorf 1983), as well as the occurrence of more general negative events such as a period in prison or overdose or the death of drug-using friends/associates (Edwards, Marshall and Cook 1997).

Ebaugh (1988) indicated the next phase in the process of role-exiting as creating the ex role. Interestingly, it seems that the potential role of formal treatment in aiding to create the ex role has been downplayed. Findings such as those of Biernacki (1986) and Sobell, Sobell, Toneatto and Leo (1993) suggest that the proportion of addicts who manage to overcome addiction without formal treatment may be even greater than or equal to the proportion who recover following treatment for their addiction.

The resolution of alcohol and drug addiction without formal treatment has been referred to as natural recovery (Havassey, Hall and Wasserman 1991), self-initiated change (Biernacki 1986), maturing out (Winick 1962), autoremission (Klingemann 1992), unassisted change

(McMurran 1994), de-addiction (Klingeman 1991), self-change (Sobell et al.1993), and self-managed change (Copeland 1998). Although a number of different terms are used, they all subscribe to the basic principle that people overcome substance abuse problems without recourse to treatment.

According to a number of research findings on the subject of natural or self recovery, natural recovery is evident from various substances. This includes alcohol (Sobell, Cunningham, and Sobell 1996), cocaine (Shaffer and Jones 1989; Waldorf, Reinarman and Murphy 1991), heroin (Biernacki 1986; Klingemann 1991, 1992; Waldorf 1983), and marijuana (Kandel and Raveis 1989).

One of the first and most widely cited descriptions of the natural recovery process of narcotic addiction is the "maturing out" theory by Winick (1962, p. 6). According to Winick, for the majority of addicts, addiction is a self-limiting process in which up to two thirds of addicts "mature out" naturally of their addiction by the time they reach their midthirties. He speculated that addicts began using narcotics in their late teens or early twenties as their method of coping with the challenges and problems present in early adulthood. Thus, by their midthirties the problems for which the addict originally began taking drugs become less significant and they "mature out" of their addiction cycle.

While it may be a fact that a large number of addicts do indeed appear to cease their addiction cycles in their midthirties (Biernacki 1986; Winick 1962), the maturation thesis is one of only several explanations of how addicts process their recovery. For example, Waldorf (1983) identifies five routes out of narcotic addiction in addition to "maturing out." Waldorf (1983) argued that individuals can also "drift" out of addiction; become alcoholic or mentally ill; give up due to religious/political conversion; "retire" by giving up the drug while retaining certain aspects of the lifestyle; or change because their situation or environment has changed.

Biernacki (1986) interviewed 101 heroin users who had overcome heroin dependence on their own. He described how a small proportion of users (5 percent) did not make a firm decision to stop using heroin. They drifted out of dependence either because of work commitments or because of lifestyle changes. A larger group (20 percent) hit rock bottom or experienced what he regarded as an existential crisis; that is, a profound emotional and psychological event that led them to question their lifestyle and identity as a heroin user. The largest group (75 percent) made a rational and explicit decision to stop using heroin either in response to an accumulation of negative experiences or because an event occurred (an overdose of a friend for example) that was particularly significant or disturbing on a personal level.

A significant number of people with drug-related problems have recovered independently of treatment (Biernacki 1986; Granfield and Cloud 1999). Waldorf et al. (1991) found that of the 106 recovering problem cocaine users in their study just over 71 percent stopped drug use without treatment.

The prevalence of untreated recovery among alcohol addicts is no less significant. In two surveys conducted in Canada, to determine the prevalence rate of recovery without treatment, Sobell et al. (1996) found that over three quarters of problem drinkers who have recovered from their problem for one year or more do so without treatment. An earlier study by Sobell et al. (1993) found that a considerable majority of alcohol abusers (82 percent) recovered on their own.

Miller (1998) and Marlatt et al. (1988) suggest that natural recoverers may not seek treatment because of preconceived attitudes and judgments toward treatment, nonconformity to these more accepted modes of rehabilitation, and a wish to avoid the labeling process (Marlatt et al. 1988). Miller (1998) and Marlatt et al. (1988) suggest that many addicts perceive themselves as having been responsible for the development of their addictions. They assume they are capable and thus have the desire to regain control of themselves on their own.

Even though research suggests that there are people who recover without the need for treatment, there is still a significant proportion that requires it. This has led to the conclusion by some that treatment is a modest but worthwhile facilitator of natural recovery. According to Edwards et al. (1997), formal treatment can be helpful in many ways that natural recovery cannot. For example, it can help to nudge the person towards a more constructive way of seeing things or enhance self-efficacy. Edwards (2000) has drawn together relevant research to provide a useful summary of how people usually get better from drinking problems and some of the ways that treatment can support recovery. First, addicts have to believe that change is feasible, and skilled therapists can be helpful in enhancing self-efficacy. Second, addicts need to be motivated, and specific treatments such as motivational interviewing can be used here. Third, since recovery involves movement towards a goal, therapists can also be helpful in clarifying appropriate goals. Next, it is clear that successful recovery involves avoiding relapse, which can be done through learning various psychological skills and with building of supportive networks, which can be achieved through groups like Alcoholics Anonymous (AA) and/or Narcotics Anonymous (NA). Finally, since change must feel good for it to be held, a major part of treatment often involves helping people to find rewarding substitutes for their use.

In conceptualizing the process of recovery from dependent alcohol or drug use, by way of natural recovery or seeking treatment help, many researchers have used the notion of a series of stages through which the individual may pass on the road to recovery (Anderson and Bondi 1998; Biernacki 1986; Ebaugh 1988; Frykholm 1985; Prochaska et al. 1992; Waldorf 1983).

As mentioned earlier, Ebaugh (1988) and Anderson and Bondi (1998) identified four stages of exiting the drug-role; first doubts, seeking alternatives, turning points and creating an ex-role. Frykholm (1985) proposed three phases of recovery from addiction; ambivalence (negative effects of drug use are increasingly felt resulting in a gradual desire to stop using drugs); treatment (attempts at detoxification become more sustained and drug-free periods grow longer); and emancipatory (addict effectively becomes an ex-addict and can remain "clean" without external assistance).

Specifically for natural recoverers, Biernacki (1986) identified four stages. The first stage is resolving to stop using. The resolution to stop is most frequently accompanied by a "rock bottom" experience or an existential crisis. The second stage is breaking away from the addiction. This involves the decision to change a lifestyle which requires modifying one's accommodation, friends and social life. The third stage is staying abstinent. This involves a relapse-prevention plan to deal with the cravings. The final stage identified by Biernacki (1986) is becoming and being ordinary. This requires dealing with the long-term changes in identity from being a member of a deviant subgroup to entering "conventional" society.

One of the most popular stage models of recovery was developed by Prochaska et al. (1992) who propose that there are five stages in the process of recovery. The first stage is precontemplation. In this stage there is no intention to change behavior in the foreseeable future. Many individuals in this stage are unaware of their problems and it is families, friends, neighbors, or employees who often pressure the addicts to enter into recovery. Usually they feel coerced into changing the addictive behavior by a spouse who threatens to leave, an employer who threatens to dismiss them, parents who threaten to disown them, or courts who threaten to punish them. They may even demonstrate change as long as the pressure is on. Once the pressure is off, however, they often quickly return to their old habits (Prochaska et al. 1992).

Contemplation is the second stage. In this stage people are aware that a problem exists and are seriously thinking about overcoming it but have not yet made a commitment to take action. People can remain stuck in the contemplation stage for long periods. An important aspect of the contemplation stage is the weighing of the pros and cons of the problem and the solution to the problem. Serious consideration of problem resolution is the central element of contemplation (Prochaska et al. 1992).

Preparation, the third stage, combines intention and behavioral criteria. Individuals in this stage are seriously intending to take action. As a group, individuals who are prepared for action report some small behavioral changes. Although they have made some reductions in their problem behaviors, individuals in the preparation stage have not yet reached a criterion for effective action, such as abstinence. They are intending, however, to take such action in the very near future (Prochaska et al. 1992).

Action is the fourth stage in which individuals modify their behavior, experiences, or environment in order to overcome their problems. Action involves the most overt behavioral changes and requires considerable commitment of time and energy. Individuals are classified in the action stage if they have successfully altered the addictive behavior for a period of one day to six months. Successfully altering the addictive behavior means reaching a particular criterion, such as abstinence (Prochaska et al. 1992).

Maintenance is the fifth and final stage in which people work to prevent relapse. Maintenance is not a static stage. Changing addictive behaviors is a continuation of change. This stage is considered to last a lifetime. Being able to remain free of the addictive behavior and being able to consistently engage in a new incompatible behavior for more than six months are the criteria for considering someone to be in the maintenance stage (Prochaska et al. 1992).

Clearly addiction and recovery are contentious and complex issues, and there is a great variation between individuals; however, there is no one single pathway into addiction or recovery.

Chapter Outlines

Chapter 2 explores the theoretical and empirical research that provides the framework for this study along with the methods used in this research. Chapter 3 considers the findings from this research providing an overview of each participant's preaddiction experiences. Chapter 4 entails the findings gleaned from the stories of the men's addicted selves. In Chapter 5, I highlight the findings from the men's recovery experiences, including how they become abstinent and resolved to live clean lives. Chapter 6 draws together my research incorporating a discussion of the lessons learned in this study including a conclusion of participants' insights into their feelings about substances now that they are in recovery. In other words, I give my participants the "last word" on the topic of addiction and recovery for them. Following these insights, thoughts on their achievements as they recovered are documented. I also offer their ideas of what recovery means to them and also what factors need to be in place for men to enter recovery including the following: individual decisions for change, the significance of a support system, and the importance of realizing that recovery is a lifelong process. Further, participants' insights into their opinions of the differences between their use/abuse of substances and that of women are offered. Finally, I conclude with participants' suggestions for change for other individuals who may be thinking of recovery coupled with my suggestions for changes in policies in the field of men's addiction and recovery processes.

2

Exploring Addiction and Recovery

The goal of this chapter is to review and identify theoretical and empirical research that highlights the research question concerning the relationship between substance abuse and individuals' selves and social identities changes, and how selves and social identities develop and transform during participants' addiction and recovery processes. Also overviewed is the particular method used in this study.

There are numerous works that consider men's addiction and recovery processes from various perspectives, but there are only a few that examine such processes within the symbolic interactionist paradigm. The following discussion elaborates briefly on early models of addiction and recovery, along with various developmental theories as they provide the groundwork for later studies. Then, I provide an overview of theorists within the symbolic interactionist perspective who have explored processes of changing selves and social identities within addiction and recovery.

Early Studies on Addiction and Recovery Processes

Early studies on addiction and recovery do not enquire into possible changes in self, changes in identity, or how people make meanings toward drug(s) of choice. These studies mainly highlight men's problems of alcoholism, and such research is based on the disease concept within the medical model (Denzin 1987a; Jellinek 1952; Stephens 1991). Little attention is paid to social problems among alcoholics, focusing, instead, on the addict, ignoring abstinence and recovery (Brown 1985). In early studies, alcohol addiction is viewed as a static state, rather than a progressive process.

The addicted individual is seen as lacking will power (Jellinek 1952) or as emotionally disturbed (Jacobs 1989). Jellinek (1952), the inventor of the modern disease concept on alcoholism, made distinctions among types of alcoholics and argued that social and economic factors were crucial to addiction processes. However, this model was based not on scientific grounds, but on moral and political grounds (Waldorf et al. 1991).

In relation to recovery processes and male heroin addicts, one early study (Winick 1962) attributed cessation to physical and psychological maturation, thus arguing that addicts mature out of addiction by their midthirties. Winick (1962) did not conduct studies with "matured-out" heroin addicts, but assumed this was the reason they stopped using. Critics (Waldorf 1983; Waldorf and Biernacki 1981) offer the view that the "maturation thesis" (McIntosh and McKeganey 2002, p. 3) is only one of many explanations of how individuals may overcome addiction. Recovery is not always self-initiated, as people are often sensitive to the concerns and pressures of others in their lives to change behaviors (Biernacki 1986; Waldorf 1983; Simpson et al. 1986). Therefore, other relevant factors need to be taken into account as individuals process recovery changes.

Other researchers (Peele 1989) argue that narcotic addiction has its source in individual and cultural constructions of experiences. This model argues that people become involved in addictive experiences, as they need a sense of power and control and to create satisfactory self-esteem. Individuals become addicted due to varying factors: social and cultural forces include social class, peer and parental influences, culture, ethnicity, stress, social support, intimacy, and positive rewards. Individual factors include choice of the addictive object, lack of values and self-restraint, health, antisocial attitudes, intolerance, uncertainty, belief in magical solutions, low self-esteem, lack of self-efficacy and external loss of control. While many of these factors may contribute to addiction processes, such an enormous amount of variables "defies the scientific canon of parsimony" (Stephens 1991, p. 119).

Consistent with early addiction models, other theories are constructed stressing a lack of control among male addicts, but also incorporate individuals' social contexts (Bacon 1973). Such social contexts include weakened social support systems, or a sense of social isolation that contributes to drinking problems. Although not based on research, Bacon (1973, p. 24) argues that recovery is a "mirror process" of addiction, as well as a "progressive phenomenon." The whole concept of recovery as a mirror image of addiction is inaccurate. Although experiences of abstinence may involve some reversal of previous failures and losses, such reversals do not automatically occur (Brown 1985). Abstinence involves the addition of new experiences, making recovery more than a mirror image or reversal. It involves a network of continuing experiences, reinforcing and building on one another. Such a model is inadequate, as it does not portray the depth and complexity of recovery (Brown 1985).

The importance of addiction as "process" is furthered through other works (Bean 1975) that theorize a progression of recovery based on changes in defensive structure, self-esteem and role. Bean (1975, p. 10) states, "[It is possible] to conceive of recovery as a process rather than a steady state, with different needs and problems at different phases." The simultaneous development of mature defenses, improved self-esteem, and object relations in one's recovery process are of importance in this early model (Bean 1975).

Other theorists (Bateson 1972) contend that a change in epistemology for the alcoholic is a necessary function in order for the individual to recover. This includes the notion of self-power as a necessity for alcoholics as they decide to leave addiction and enter recovery. Bateson (1972) argues that a conversion is in play among former addicts that includes moving away from symmetric, competitive relationships with the world to complementary stances in which individuals see themselves as part of a larger whole. However, if it is argued that the self of the user is at the core of the addiction process, then, the struggle is with self, not with others (Denzin 1987a). Therefore, this study (Bateson 1972) does not provide an understanding of the dialectics of men's inner and outer experiences with themselves, alcohol, and others (Denzin 1987a).

While the above researchers/theorists may differ in some particulars, there is a commonality in the various works: emerging sociocultural approaches to addiction and recovery processes (Stephens 1991). Although the paradigm of symbolic interactionism is not of consideration among early scholars, early studies hint at a sense of movement and change within addicts' lives and are a beginning to further understanding the possible progression of addiction and recovery among substance abusers.

Addiction and Recovery Processes: The Symbolic Interactionist Perspective

As indicated earlier, the traditional function of symbolic interactionism is to offer a theory of self, interaction, and socialization, which speaks to the question of how individuals are formed out of the interaction order (Denzin 1992). Interactionists assume that individuals create the world of experiences they live in. They do this by acting on things in terms of the meanings things have for them (Blumer 1969). These meanings come from interactions, and they are shaped by self-reflections individuals bring to situations. Such self-interaction "is interwoven with social interaction and influences that social interaction" (Blumer 1981, p. 153).

Symbolic interaction (the merger of self and social interaction) is the chief means, "by which human beings are able to form social or joint acts" (Blumer 1981, p. 153). Joint acts, their formations, dissolutions, conflicts and mergers constitute the social life of a human society. Society consists of the joint or social acts that are formed and carried out by members (Blumer 1981; Denzin 1992).

Symbolic interactionists place strong emphasis on the ways in which identities are forged contextually and through actual processes of interaction during which selves are named (Stone 1962; Turner 1978; Zurcher 1977). Therefore, researchers within the symbolic interactionist tradition who are addiction/recovery researchers locate addiction, not in the drug(s), but in the relationship of the addict to self, to the drug(s) and with others (Denzin 1987a). The following discussion highlights varying attributes of changing individual selves and social identities as expressed by theorists within the fields of addiction and recovery applicable to this study.

One of the early studies on addiction through the symbolic interactionism perspective is highlighted in Becker's (1953) classical study on how male respondents make meaning of marijuana usage. I make singular note of Becker's (1953) work, as his research with marijuana users is a classic in the addiction field. Using Mead's (1934) discussion of the meaning of social objects in his classic text, *Mind, Self and Society*, Becker (1953) constructs a theory of marijuana addiction through his interviews with 50 men who narrate their use of this drug. Becker (1953) focuses on the history of men's experiences, major changes that occur in attitudes toward experiences, actual usage, along with reasons for changes into addiction.

Becker (1953) argues that marijuana use develops in the course of one's experiences while using this drug. Marijuana use has to do with "a sequence of social experiences during which the person acquires a conception of the meaning of the behavior, and perceptions and judgments of objects and situations, all of which make the activity possible and desirable" (Becker 1953, p. 235). He further states:

> Most frequently a curiosity about the kind of experience the drug will produce – are transformed into definite patterns of action through the social interpretation of a physical experience. Marijuana use is a function of the individual's conception of marijuana and of the uses to

which it can be put, and this conception develops as the individual's experience with the drug increases. (1953, p. 42)

In this work, Becker (1953) argues that a sequence of changes in attitudes and experiences lead one to use marijuana for pleasure. He further states that psychological explanations are not in themselves sufficient to account for marijuana use. Nor can psychological traits account for the variability over time of a given individual's behavior with reference to the drug. Becker (1953, p. 4) states that it is impossible to explain addiction using a theory based on the user's need for "escape," but it is possible to understand an addict's use if there is a consideration of how the individual changes in how he makes meaning of the drug he is using, similar to this study's focus. As well, even though Becker (1953) did not consider recovery per se in this work, it can be argued that a similar process is in play in recovery processes. This implies that individuals can learn that they are capable of alternate activities, not related to drug use/abuse and, eventually, find pleasure in these pursuits (Maruna 2001).

Becker (1953) argues that a comparison of the character of the drug experience has its roots in Mead's (1934) theory of the self and the relation of objects to the self. Objects have meaning for the person only as he imputes meaning to them in the course of his interaction with them. The meaning is not given in the object, but is lodged there as the person acquires a conception of the kind of action that can be taken with, toward, by and for it. Meanings arise in the course of social interaction, deriving their character from the consensus participants develop about the object in question.

Similar to Becker's work (1953) is Lindesmith's (1968) concept of self in his major theory of addiction within the symbolic interactionist paradigm with male opiate users. Lindesmith's (1968) study consisted of 65 individuals who were mostly male, White, lower class, and had criminal arrests and criminal records (Keys and Galliher 2000). Lindesmith (1968, p. 91) described his theory of addiction "as an essential process of transformation, using of the social symbols of language in conversation with oneself and others." Lindesmith (1968, p. 193) related this directly to Mead's (1934) taking the role of the generalized other where the addict adopts the attitudes of the addict group. For Lindesmith (1968), addiction was one of the situations made possible by language and conceptual thought (Keys and Galliher 2000). Lindesmith (1968, p. 95) argues:

The effect which the biological events associated with using drugs has on human behavior is seen as one that is mediated by the manner in which such events are perceived or conceptualized by the person who experiences them ... . As the user applies to his own experiences and behavior the attitudes, symbols and sentiments current in his society, he is faced with a problem of adjusting himself to the unpleasant implications of being an addict ... . In his efforts to rationalize his own conduct, which he cannot understand or justify, and to make it more tolerable to himself, he is drawn to others like himself.

A major element of Lindesmith's (1968) addiction theory concerns the self-concept of the addict, which is totally centered on drug use (Keys and Galliher 2000). The addict's self-concept is central to addiction. Lindesmith (1968) pointed to the importance of one's physical addiction to narcotics and the association of withdrawal distress to the formation of the self-concept of narcotic addiction and to the formation of an addict subculture.

Following Becker's (1953) work on meaning making and Lindesmith's (1968) work on the concept of self, studies have evolved in intervening years that consider varying characteristics of addiction/recovery processes within the symbolic interactionist perspective.

A number of studies (Anderson 1991; Denzin 1987a; Haas 2003) have indicated that an altered sense of identity or a dissociative-like state (Jacobs 1989) occurs in an individual's life that predisposes them to addiction. Denzin (1987a, p. 21) argues that the addicted individual (self) uses drugs to escape an "inner emptiness of self." This emptiness can be manifested in a fundamental instability of self-experience. The individual seeks transcendence from how they see their reality, and addiction becomes the "fix" for the emotional pain (Haas 2003, p. 36). Therefore, it can be argued that addiction is used as a crutch; as a means of finding a valued self-feeling that will transcend the inner lack that is felt on a regular basis. In other words, drugs are used as an anesthetic to escape from deep problematics of the self as the individual becomes fixated on the ritual and object of their addiction (Haas 2003, Denzin 1987a).

According to Anderson (1991), a sense of identity discomfort occurs in addicts' lives. This approach argues that drug use/abuse initially alleviates respondents' existing identity discomforts that arise from a myriad of mostly micro factors. Micro factors such as one's self-concept, one's level of personal satisfaction and one's personal control are all linked to one's relationship to drugs. Therefore, drug euphorias deliver much more than personal pleasure from altered states. They also help the addict create a new version of the self that is much more desirable than the old (Anderson 1991; Maruna 2001).

A sense of a hated self is also believed to develop in addiction processes (Anderson 1991; Denzin 1987a; Haas 2003; Jacobs 1989). In these studies, the self of the user lies at the core of the addiction process, thus, addiction may be understood as one's avoidance of intimacy with a hated self (Peele 1989). Such a sense of self-loathing can be characterized as internal progression (Ebaugh 1988), ultimately leading to the alienation of one's self in an addict's life (Haas 2003). This alienation of self, as Haas (2003) and Denzin argue (1987a), compels addicts to create "functional identities" which resituates them. Such "functional identities" bring with them new scripts for action for addicts: the pursuit of drugs, drug using friendships and drug lifestyles.

Addiction scholars (Granfield and Cloud 1999; Haas 2003; Murphy and Rosenbaum 1999) also make note of the self that arises out of the emotional pain derived from childhood experiences. This sense of self evolves out of the perceived appraisal of others. For example, Haas (2003) argues that most addicts retrospectively interpret their childhoods as difficult, where they felt like they "didn't belong" or they were "different." In this case, addiction can be seen as a dependent state acquired over time by an individual in their attempt to relieve such chronic stresses or strain conditions (Kiecolt 1994; Haas 2003). Such childhood experiences that produce a deep sense of personal inadequacy and rejection can predispose an individual to addiction (Haas 2003; Taber 1993), due to ego identity discomfort and a felt loss of control in defining an identity (Anderson 1991).

Therefore, one's addictive behavior can be viewed as the result of shifts in self experiences (Haas 2003; Kiecolt 1994; Shaffer 1996). Such situations can occur within the context of primary relationships and, as such, gives "rise to perceptions that provide formative and lasting awareness and definitions of self" (Haas 2003, p. 109). "Addiction can, then, be understood as symptomatic behavior – a temporary and ultimately problem-filled solution" (Haas 2003, p. 61) applicable to stressful conditions in individuals' lives.

Additional research on the rebuilding of the self is of consideration in other studies (Becker 1960; Biernacki 1986). In order for a rebuilding of the self to occur, a deconstruction, or destruction of the alcoholically divided self (Denzin 1987a; Haas 2003) and a conversion and commitment to a new way of life (Becker 1960) must occur. As an individual enters recovery, not only is there a self-change, but also an identity transformation (Anderson 1991; Biernacki 1986), or an "alternation" (Travisano 1970, p. 606), oftentimes described as "a radical reorganization of identity, meaning, and life" (Travisano 1970, p. 535). It is the process of changing one's sense of root reality (Heirich 1977).

Researchers (Lofland 1966; Lofland and Stark 1965; Straus 1976) argue that, typically, a conversion is an active process through which individuals give up one way of life for another, and it implies that the convert renounces his former life patterns. Such a conversion involves the addict attempting to manage their "spoiled identity" (Goffman 1963, p. 19) that they gained in addiction. This "spoiled identity" can be related to one's former "master role" (Ebaugh 1988, p. 203), which consists of one's role as an addict. Individuals in recovery attempt to reassume unspoiled identities, or revert to previous identities. That is, addicts may revise or augment their former unspoiled identities (Biernacki 1986).

Further, other scholars (Biernacki 1986; Copeland 1998; Ettorre 1992; Murphy and Rosenbaum 1999; Rosenbaum 1981) add to the literature by suggesting that a "spoiled identity" (Goffman 1963, p. 19) comes about when the user's addict identity conflicts with, and creates problems for, other identities that are unrelated to drug use, such as partner (i.e., wife), parent (i.e., father), or employee, in ways that are unacceptable to the user. According to Brown (1985), Ebaugh (1988) and Biernacki (1986), a life event, or a "turning point" (Brown 1985, p. 33) is experienced, resulting in the feeling that if one does not change, something of value may be lost (i.e., one's child or one's health). According to Biernacki (1986, p. 53)

> Some addicts ... resolve to change their lives and stop using opiates when the option of continuing to use drugs entails consequences that are simply far too undesirable in terms of their view they have of themselves and their future lives. At this point, they rationally weigh each possibility and decide that they have much more to gain by breaking the addiction than by continuing it.

In order to recover, an addict must establish another identity, and another role (i.e., nonaddict) in order to enter into different social relationships (McMahon 1995). Individuals must also make conscious efforts to shut out the addict world and commit to more conventional activities (Biernacki 1986).

Using a developmental model in her work, Brown (1985) argues that addiction is characterized by change in the kind of focus seen by the individual but not the focus itself. The other two components, environmental interactions and interpretation of self and others change in content and process depending on interactions with the other two components (Brown 1985). In this sense, the addictive role is more than a role (Brown 1985; Denzin 1987a; Haas 2003). It is a new identity that forms the core of new behaviors, attitudes, and beliefs. Researchers signify that this core of new behavior represents what Stephens (1991, p. 260) calls "role engulfment." This role constitutes one's "master status" (Becker 1963, p. 35). Such a status overrides all other statuses enabling addicts to integrate addictive identities and its attendant statuses into one's self-concept. It denotes a constellation of roles organized around and through one salient identity. This engulfment can also involve recovery from various situations, specifying a significant transformation of identity in which new meanings, practices, and associations achieve saliency over less valued ones (Denzin 1987b).

Building on previous works, McIntosh and McKeganey (2002) suggest that identities that have been seriously damaged by addiction and the addictive lifestyle can stimulate addicts "to restore their identities and establish a different kind of future for themselves" (p. 152). When addicts recognize the extent to which their selves have been degraded, and resolve to change for that reason, then successful recovery is possible. Therefore, key to the recovery process lies in the realization by addicts that their damaged sense of selves have to be restored, combined with a reawakening of old identities and/or the establishment of new ones (Biernacki 1986: McIntosh and McKeganey 2002). This is an occurrence whereby the identity as an addict becomes "de-emphasized (symbolically and socially) relative to other identities existing or emerging as part of persons' overall life arrangement" (Biernacki 1986, p. 25). Within recovery, the individual becomes a "deployable agent" (Lofland and Stark 1965, p. 862), or total convert to their change.

A common thread or theme unites the above mentioned studies: self and self-changes are fundamental in both addiction and recovery processes. These studies argue that there is a significant transformation of self and identity in addiction along with a rebuilding of self in recovery in which new meanings, practices, and associations achieve saliency over less valued ones (Denzin 1987b; Van Den Bergh 1991). As Denzin (1987a, p. 51) argues

A theory of addiction (and relapse) cannot explain addiction or relapse solely in terms of the effects that the drug in question produces for the user. Not only are such explanations tautological, and hence untestable, but they fail to locate the key factor in addiction, which is the user's symbolic and interactional relationship with the drug. The self of the user lies at the core of the addiction process.

Addiction, then, involves three causal agents: the self of the user, his or her physiological and lived body and the drug in question (Denzin 1987a). Conversely, Brown (1985, p. 55) makes note of recovery:

At its core, the alcoholism recovery process is one of construction and reconstruction of a person's fundamental identity and resultant view of the world. The proposed dynamic model of alcoholism is, therefore, primarily a developmental model of knowledge construction and reconstruction.

Thus, recovery turns on a dialogue between two self-structures: the old self of the past and the new self of recovery, incorporating a new identity as part of the process (Denzin 1987a). Reconstruction of individuals' selves and identities are parts of the process.

Quitting drug abuse can also mean that individuals undergo an "existential crisis" (Biernacki 1986, p. 25), meaning that addicts experience profound emotional and psychological changes. In such self changes, former addicts have reached the nadir of their lives and decide that addictive lifestyles are intolerable, thus believing that one's true self is not compatible with the addict self-concept (Stephens 1991). Abstinence occurs for others as they have burned out, are tired of the life, the changes, of other junkies, and of going to jail. Obviously, such individuals are experiencing role strain – a felt inability to continue to enact the requirements of the addict role and lifestyle (Biernacki 1986).

Building on the symbolic interactionism paradigm within addiction and recovery processes that considers self, other and social object, scholars (Rudy 1986; Stephens 1991) argue that becoming addicted and the type of addict one becomes has as much to do with the responses of others as it does with the using activities and life experiences of the addict. Such responses of others refer to one's reference group. Reference groups provide generalized others to an individual whereby one can refer their conduct and against whose standards their conduct is evaluated. In addiction, reference groups are important to addicts as they provide socialization into addictive roles, motivation for assuming certain roles, and feedback to how addicts are enacting their roles (Stephens 1991).

Addiction processes involve factors of a reference group nature, that is, processes of heroin addiction operate through the process of social interaction with other heroin users (Stephens 1991). This signifies that social behavior develops not only as we respond to the expectations of others and as we experience their norms, but also through the processes of social interaction with others (Stephens 1991). Stephens (1991, p. xi) argues

> The addicts' self-concept, their sense of personal worth and their status in the addict subculture all revolve around this role of being a street addict.

In this sense, addicts' sense of selves revolves around a reference group of other users. Reference groups are also applicable to one's self-concept and identity changes in recovery processes. Changing self-concepts are related to one's reference groups and one's interpretations of situations and events (Terry 2003). Recovering addicts who are trying to do good will benefit by developing new relationships and self-concepts that either exclude or depreciate their old values (Terry 2003). Obviously, we derive a sense of self from reflected appraisals of reference groups and significant others in our lives.

Strategies are important to individuals as they change their sense of selves in recovery processes for several scholars (Denzin 1987b; Terry 2003). Strategies, such as help through one's relationships, combined with a sense of connection to one's reference groups are of importance to recovering addicts. If, as scholars (Denzin 1987b; Stephens 1991: Terry 2003) argue, recovery requires a rebuilding of self, then such meanings of self and related processes of self-change occur interactionally within a complex web of social relations. Inevitably, it can be argued that one's strategy of action is contingent on the help available for the individual in change processes. Such structural supports can consist of AA recovery programs, self-help literature, and mental health professionals, among others. Recovering addicts strongly identify with one another because of their shared problem – alcoholism and addiction – and their shared goal – sobriety or clean time (Terry 2003). Many individuals come to see AA and/or NA members as their family and they become "connected" to the group. Social support for self-change is related positively to the decision for changing oneself. Another's approval can accelerate one's decision to change (Ebaugh 1988). In this sense, recovery can only be accomplished through one's own efforts with assistance of others who have traveled the same pathways (Stephens 1991).

Additional research (Biernacki 1986; McIntosh and McKeganey 2002; Waldorf 1983) on the significance of others in recovery processes suggests that recovery from addiction is a phenomenon in which addicts must develop new relationships that help them forge new or residual roles that are circular to the processes of identity transformations. New activities and relationships are vital to the establishment of new identities. They supply former addicts with "identity materials" (McIntosh and McKeganey 2002, p. 156) from which they can build and sustain new selves. Recovery can be understood as an ongoing process of interaction through which people adopt new meanings and new self-images (Granfield and Cloud 1999). It is also "a process that requires some effort and invariably demands some form of behavioral plan for its successful completion" (Copeland 1998, p. 41).

Obviously, then, along with one's reference groups, the influence of significant others is important in an individual's decision to stop their use/abuse of controlled substances (Frykholm 1985; Simpson et al. 1986; Smart 1994; Waldorf 1983). Most importantly, the influence of families, children and/or partners relates to the importance of "bridging" (Ebaugh 1988, p. 147) among former addicts. Such "bridging" (Ebaugh 1988, p. 147) incorporates the process of reestablishing relationships with friends, family, hobbies, or jobs. People with bridges establish new identities and new roles as nonaddicts more easily (Ebaugh 1988; Granfield and Cloud 1999, Stephens 1991; Snow 1997). "Bridging" (Ebaugh 1988, p. 147) involves a connection to others, thus allowing the person to see himself as part of the larger whole once again (Brown 1985; Denzin 1987b; Granfield and Cloud 1999). It is a moving away from isolation to building dependence on other objects in one's life (Brown 1985).

Building on addiction and recovery processes within the symbolic interactionist paradigm, researchers (Biernacki 1986; Brown 1985; Denzin 1987b; McIntosh and McKeganey 2002) suggest that as individuals become addicted, meanings toward controlled substances change as drugs become functional for the user. As Blumer (1969, p. 68) argues, meaning "is not intrinsic to the object." Each object changes for us, not because it changes, but because we change our definitions. The drug in question for each user, then, provides consistent support for the addict. It is, as Brown (1985, p. 136) suggests, "a buddy, a constant companion." For users, it becomes the primary object of their intense dependency.

Conversely, in recovery, meanings change again as drugs no longer have the same meaning as they once did for the user. The addict defines their relationship to controlled substances (Denzin 1987a) in this manner in both addiction and recovery processes. It can be argued that there is a symmetrical struggle with one's drug(s) of choice, the social object to which respondents pay attention as they become addicted and, then, in recovery. In alcohol studies (and in other drug studies) the drug in question is the meaningful social object that brings comfort and pleasure to the drinker (Denzin 1987a, b). In addiction, then, the social objects, controlled substances, secure a lifestyle that is meaningful within the use/abuse of drugs for the addict. And, consequently, the alcoholic's other relationships (Denzin 1987a) produce experiences that solidify this meaning among users.

Additional research (Brown 1985, 162) suggests that one of the most important changes that occur in recovery is the shift in "object attachment." The addict is primarily attached to their drug(s) of choice in addiction. In recovery, the individual needs to relinquish their drug(s) as a substance and an object of attachment. Substitution for the former use/abuse of controlled substances is a necessary component in recovery – something has to replace the addict's object of desire. Within AA and/or NA programs, such substitution may involve the organization itself, and/or individuals who are part of such programs. Strategies need to be put in place in former addicts' lives in order to "manage one's desire" (McIntosh and McKeganey 2002, p. 125) for the former drug(s) of choice. One meaningful strategy is "negative contexting" (McIntosh and McKeganey 2002, p. 126; Biernacki 1986) which involves former drug addicts remembering the negative side of using drugs. Overall, one's new life is being built with new activities, new commitments and relationships, thus providing new materials for dealing with unwelcome thoughts by such means as distraction or "negative contexting."

What the above studies suggest is that not only is the self of consideration in addiction and recovery processes, but also what is salient are important others and how individuals change their meanings toward their substances(s) of choice. The foregoing studies provide important insights into these important concepts within addiction and recovery processes.

The foregoing discussion illustrates that many scholars (Brudenell 1997; Denzin 1987a, b; Haas 2003; Van den Bergh 1991) argue that addiction and recovery are processes that occur over time and involve psychological, physical, cognitive, emotional, and spiritual changes. These processes involve both internal and external changes; they are continuous processes that do not take place in a vacuum (Abbott 1995; Denzin 1987b; Underhill 1991) and involve conscious changes in individuals' life directions (Smith 1991).

Further, addiction and recovery from addiction are phenomena in which addicts develop new relationships that help them forge new or residual roles that are circular to the processes of identity transformations. Such transformations can be understood as ongoing processes of interaction through which people adopt new meanings and new self-images (Granfield and Cloud 1999). As Biernacki (1986, p. 25) argues

> Recovery refers to the process through which a new calculus or arrangement of identities and perspectives emerges and becomes relatively stabilized. This process entails a different articulation of identities in which the identity as an addict becomes de-emphasized (both symbolically and socially) relative to other identities existing or emerging as part of the person's overall life arrangement.

Such meanings and related processes of self-change occur interactionally within complex webs of social relations (Van den Bergh 1991). Self and identity are always product and process, embodying continuity and change (Josselson 1996).

This chapter section has presented a review of the theoretical and empirical research that highlights the relationship between substance abuse and individuals' selves and social identities changes, and how selves and social identities can develop and transform during recovery processes. The following section considers the methods used in this research study.

Methods

A qualitative method together with the paradigm of symbolic interaction is employed for this research study. My analysis centers on the following questions that consider the various ways in which participants interact with selves, others, and controlled substances as they take on identities as addicts and, eventually, as recovered addicts: What do addiction and recovery mean to men formerly addicted? How do they explain their addiction? What do they think enabled them to enter recovery?

> We know the world through the stories that are told about it. (Denzin and Lincoln 2008, p. 45)

As Denzin and Lincoln (2008) argue in the above quote, my objective in this research was to uncover participants' stories that they relayed to me regarding their addiction and recovery experiences, enhancing our understanding of their "worlds" of drug use/abuse. Prince (2000 [1990], p. 129) also states that

> to study the nature of narratives, to examine how and why it is that we can construct them, memorise them, paraphrase them, summarize and expand them, or organize them in terms of such categories as plot, narrator, narratee, and character is to study one of the fundamental ways – and a singularly human one at that – in which we *make* sense.

People without narratives do not exist: life itself must be considered a narrative inside which we find a number of other stories (Moen 2006). Vygotsky (1978) argues that how people become what they are depends on what they have experienced in the social contexts in which they have participated. Narratives capture both the individual and the context (Moen 2006).

The qualitative approach links with symbolic interactionism as the qualitative method requires access to participants' meanings in this research study. One can get at meaning through close-ended kinds of data collection techniques, but one must interview and/or observe in order to know the social objects that provide meaning to participants. Processual analysis is possible quantitatively, but such an approach requires a good prior grasp of relevant variables. In this study, an exploratory analysis is called for. For example, what the researcher learns from one participant's interview may lead her/him to either rethink a specific interview or to add more participants.

Walker (1985) argues that

> Qualitative researchers have helped us to understand and demystify drug taking, dispel unhelpful myths and stereotypes about drug users, build and develop theories of addiction and formulate and evaluate drug policy and practice. They have also had particular advantages in studying hidden and hard-to-reach groups, identifying emerging trends in drug consumption and researching particularly sensitive drug issues. (p. 22)

Denzin and Lincoln (2008, p. 4) maintain that "qualitative research is a situated activity that locates the observer in the world. It consists of a set of interpretive, material practices that make the world visible." Qualitative techniques are highly effective in researching sensitive and/or illegal activities—hence substance use and misuse in general, but particularly very sensitive drug-related issues. Similarly, qualitative researchers' sensitivity to the socialand cultural specificity of their study population can foster an awareness and empathy that encourages those being researched to disclose their vulnerabilities (Neale, Allen and Coombes 2005).

Further, qualitative researchers study things in their natural settings, attempting to make sense of, or interpret, phenomena in terms of the meanings people bring to them. As Stanley and Temple (2008) argue, "Lives are always 'read' and interpreted through the stories told, and untold, about them" (p. 278). Overall, qualitative researchers seek answers to questions that stress how social experience is created and given meaning (Denzin and Lincoln 2008). Therefore, following Denzin and Lincoln (2008), this study calls for a flexible, qualitative design.

We act toward our environment according to our ongoing definitions arising from our perspectives (Charon 2001). Charon (2001, p. 40) further contends that

> Symbolic interactionism regards the individual as active in the environment; an organism that interacts with others and with self; a dynamic being; a being that defines immediate situations according to perspectives developed and altered in ongoing social interactions.

Stanley and Temple (2008, p. 276) claim that "narratives are always contextual, communal and relational."We do not simply respond to our environments, but we define, act toward it, and use it. The function of symbolic interactionism is to offer a theory of self, interaction, and socialization, which speaks to the question of how human beings are formed out of the interaction order (Denzin 1992). As Blumer (1969) argues, meanings come from interaction and such meanings are shaped by the self-reflections persons bring to situations. Self-interaction is interwoven with social interaction and influences that social interaction. "Human beings are purposeful, goal-seeking, feeling, meaning-attributing and meaning-responding creatures" (Hughes 1976, p. 24). Consequently, it is necessary tounderstand how they perceive and interpret their environment if their behavior is ever to be interpreted usefully.

George Herbert Mead (1934,1938) is the first theorist to lay the foundation for the symbolic interactionism approach as he considers the notion that human group life is the essential condition for "the emergences of consciousness, the mind, the world of objects, human beings as organisms possessing selves, and human conduct in the form of constructed acts" (Blumer 1969: p. 61). In developing this approach, Mead (1934) explains how these phenomena emerge through the processes of interaction and communication (Sandstrom, Martin and Fine 2003). While naming Mead (1934) as the founder of interactionism, authoritative statements regarding symbolic interactionism are found in the writings of Herbert Blumer (1969). He moved the central theoretical and empirical concerns of merely observable human behavior to the symbolic transformation of that behavior through meanings, along with cognitive processes of interpretation through which the transformation takes place and is integrated into human interaction (Weigert, Tiege and Tiege 1986).

Blumer (1969) argues that the central insight of interactionist theory is that all behaviors, emotions, beliefs, rules, and objects become meaningful within the broader social context of interaction with others. This perspective views the individual as an ever-changing actor: communicating, role taking, cooperating, and problem solving in a "stream of action" (Charon 2001, p. 124). Symbolic interactionism regards the human being as active in their environment; a being that defines situations according to perspectives developed and altered in ongoing social interaction. As meanings are understood in processual terms and as being sustained in and through social relationships, this perspective is especially suited to the study of changes in meaning as social relationships change (McMahon 1995). For this reason, the symbolic interactionist perspective helps inform the experiences for participants in this study. Such an approach enables me to scrutinize symbolic action and sociocultural meanings enacted in such actions as appropriate subject matters on men's addiction and recovery processes.

For this research study it is important to provide an overview of the setting and context of the study. As Corbin and Strauss (2008) argue "any explanation of experience would be incomplete without locating experience within the larger conditional frame or context in which it is embedded" (p. 17). The following discussion highlights this important factor.

Background and Context of the Study

In the state of Missouri where this research study took place, the impact of substance abuse on state government is substantial: in the neighborhood of $1.3 billion annually (Missouri Department of Mental Health (MDMH) 2008). Overall, societal costs for Missouri are estimated at $7 billion (MDMH 2008). According to the National Survey on Drug Use and Health (NSDUH), an estimated 477,000 individuals in Missouri have alcohol or illicit drug dependence or abuse within the past year, representing roughly 10 percent of the state's population. About 60 percent of those with a substance abuse problem are male (SAMHSA 2005, 2006). Nonabusers are impacted by drug and alcohol-related crime, motor vehicle crashes, taxes to pay for incarceration and rehabilitation services, and increased insurance premiums (Missouri Division of Alcohol and Drug Abuse, MDADA, 2008, p.3).

Alcohol is by far the most common substance problem for those entering treatment followed by marijuana, cocaine, methamphetamine, and heroin. Geographically, marijuana is well represented in both rural and urban areas. Methamphetamine is prominent in the rural areas – in particular, the southwest region including Joplin, Springfield, and Branson – as well as in the Kansas City area. Haight, Jacobsen, Black, Kingery, Sheridan, Mulder (2005) argue that methamphetamine has historically been a rural phenomenon with use and production generally higher in rural areas than urban (Herz 2000). As well, the methamphetamine market in Missouri differs greatly between the eastern and western halves of the state. The western half of the state is dominated by crystal "ice" methamphetamine, supplied by organizations based out of Mexico, California, and the southwest United States, and transported to the area by the traditional highway transportation organizations (Drug Enforcement Administration 2009). Historically, overall, Missouri has been known as a methamphetamine-producing state (MDADA, 2008). Further, cocaine is highly concentrated in the urban areas – Kansas City and St Louis – as well as Columbia and Springfield. Heroin is noticeably concentrated in the St Louis area (MDADA, 2008, p. 9).

According to 2004-2007 data from the NSDUH, approximately 0.8 percent of persons aged 12 or older in Missouri reported using methamphetamine within the past year (SAMHSA 2004, 2005, 2006, and 2007). Results of a 2007 survey of Missouri students show that approximately 2.9 percent of ninth graders, 2.3 percent of tenth graders, 4.6 percent of eleventh graders, and 4.7 percent of twelfth graders reported using methamphetamine at least once during their lifetimes (Youth Online Comprehensive Results 2008).

Substance abuse and crime are closely linked. In a survey of state prisons, the Bureau of Justice found that 32 percent of inmates committed their offense under the influence of drugs, and 17 percent committed their crime to obtain money for drugs (MDADA, 2008, p. 12). Further, costs to local and state government are certainly felt by the criminal justice system as well as social programs designed to ameliorate the damage caused by substance abuse and addiction. Each year, Missouri state government spends an estimated $1.3 billion on the burden resulting from substance abuse, or about $245 per Missourian (MDADA 2008). Much of the cost to state government – nearly half – deals with criminal behavior brought about by substance abuse. The impact on Missouri's justice system is significant. At midyear 2006,

Missouri's institutional population totaled 30,825 offenders with another 69,165 under supervised probation or parole. About 23 percent of the offenses resulting in incarceration are directly related to drugs and driving under the influence (MDADA 2008, p. 5).

This, however, does not include all crimes committed while under the influence of alcohol and drugs. Substance abuse is often a contributing factor in property crime and assaults due to impaired judgment and the need to obtain money to buy drugs. Past surveys of state and federal inmates found that nearly one-third reported having used drugs at the time of their offense (MDADA 2008, p. 7).

Clearly, substance abuse and addiction have a tremendous impact on the lives of Missourians, burdening individuals, families, communities, and government with the negative consequences which include property theft, motor vehicle crashes, school failure, low worker productivity, family dysfunction, and homelessness. This impact is felt by individuals and families of every ethnic group and in every tax bracket (MDADA 2008, p. 6).

The following section provides an overview of the data collection methods, along with a summation of the men's backgrounds.

Methods of Data Collection

The analytical technique used in this study features a qualitative design with a semi-structured, open-ended interview schedule and a self-selective technique with 25 men who self-identify as being formerly addicted, who are 20 years of age or older, and who have been in recovery for 18 months or longer. The grounded theory method enables me to analyze the qualitative data and to develop theoretical categories regarding the general processes of men's addiction and recovery, inclusive of their personal accounts of their experiences.

The grounded theory method is useful for this study as my focus is on the individual man's experiences regarding underlying patterns or commonalities, inconsistencies, intended and unintended consequences of action, meaning systems, assumptions they hold, and social systems and interactions that are part of their behavior (Ebaugh 1988; Karp, Butler and Bergsdtram 1998). Further, grounded theory offers "'avenues for broadening our understanding of how human beings make sense of their worlds and choose to behave in response to particular life circumstances'" (Benoliel 2001, p. 1).

The sampling design used in this study was purposive sampling. Purposive sampling looks for representativeness by choosing a sample that typifies the population, the theoretical category, or the phenomenon that is to be studied (Denzin and Lincoln 2008). The sample design in this study was chosen to enable me to investigate typical phenomena pertaining to theoretical issues of processes of these particular men's addiction and recovery processes.[1] Posters about the project were placed in public places, such as restaurants, local hotels for men, local grocery stores, community malls, churches, and local gathering places in the community. Participants were free to call me and offer to be interviewed. In order to participate in the study, participants had to meet the following inclusion criteria as they were asked the following questions: what is your age now; at what age did you begin to use drugs, what types of drugs did you use, how long have you had problems with drugs and/or alcohol, and how long have you been in recovery from your use of drugs and/or alcohol? If my callers met these inclusion criteria, they were invited to be interviewed by me.

Many men interviewed were acquired through the snowball sampling technique, that is, men I had previously interviewed recommended the study to others they knew, resulting in other participants contacting me. In other words, this type of sampling is a carefully staged process that involves the recruitment of new respondents through referrals from earlier respondents (Neale et al. 2005). Participants were paid $25.00 for their time.

The interview for participants was approximately 1-2 hours in length. The interview length was not set by the interviewer but depended on how long each participant was willing to discuss his recovery process. The history of their drug and/or alcohol use and their recovery experiences were the two themes used throughout the interview (see Appendix for the questionnaire). When appropriate, interviewees were asked to elaborate on their comments.

Men's Backgrounds

Table 2.1 illustrates the men's demographic backgrounds. Their ages ranged between 24 and 58, with a median age of 39. Of the 25 men interviewed, 13 signified that their ethnic background was White and of English origin. Seven were of Native American descent, and five were Black. As well, nine of the men stated that they came from Norwegian, Russian, Dutch, German and Irish backgrounds. Although all participants lived in the study area where the interviews took place, few were born in the area. For example, seven of the participants were born

---

1. REB consent was acquired and ethical standards were complied with throughout the research process.

and raised in the city where the research was completed, while three were from St. Louis and one from Kansas City. Five of the men came from small towns in Missouri; eight were from other parts of the United States while one was born in another country and he had moved to the United States while he was a child. All participants identified themselves as heterosexual in orientation.

Table 2.1. Participants' Personal Backgrounds

Variables	Frequency percent	(n)
Age		
20–29	20.0	(5)
30–39	36.0	(9)
40–49	28.0	(7)
50+	16.0	(4)
Marital status		
Single	24.0	(6)
Married	48.0	(12)
Common law	4.0	(1)
Divorced	20.0	(5)
Widowed	4.0	(1)
Highest education attained		
High school	28.0	(7)
Community college	40.0	(10)
Some university	24.0	(6)
Completed university	8.0	(2)
Ethnic group		
White	52.0	(13)
Black, African, Caribbean	20.0	(5)
Native American	28.0	(7)
Religious affiliation		
Protestant	44.0	(11)
Catholic	8.0	(2)
Other	28.0	(7)
None	20.0	(5)

Table 2.1. Participants' Personal Backgrounds (cont'd)

Variables	Frequency percent	(n)
Occupation		
Professional	8.0	(2)
Service employee	60.0	(15)
No occupation	24.0	(6)
Student	8.0	(2)
Net income		
$0–9,999	36.0	(9)
$10,000–19,999	12.0	(3)
$20,000–29,999	32.0	(8)
$30,000–39,999	20.0	(5)
(n) = 25		

As most of the participants came from other areas of either the state and/or other parts of the United States, and in order to protect the participants' anonymity/confidentiality, place-as-context in this research study is not featured exclusively. Such a stance also helps in highlighting more clearly the stories of these men relative to their addiction and recovery processes.

At the time of the interviews, six of the men were single, 12 were married, five were divorced, one was living common law, and one was widowed. Eighteen of the men had children, while seven had none. The number of children varied, between one and six in number. Their children's ages varied, from two years of age to 29.

The highest education obtained by seven participants was high school. Ten men had graduated from a local community college. Six participants had some university education, while two had completed university. Seventeen men were working when interviewed whereas six stated that they had no work and two participants were students. Participants worked in such diverse areas as construction, driving trucks, line cooks, factory work, janitor work, debris hauling, substance abuse counselor, and waiting tables. Participants' employment was linked with income: the income of the nine not employed fell below $10,000 (US) per year. Three men had earned between $10,000 and $19,999 in the prior year, while the remainder (n=13) had incomes between $20,000 and $39,999.

Religious affiliation varied among participants: 11 were Protestant, two were of the Catholic faith, and seven signified that they had no religious affiliation. The remaining men (n=5) stated that they practiced in the Islam, Pentecostal, and/or Lutheran faith and one is a Wiccan.

Summary

This chapter reviewed and identified the theoretical and empirical research that highlighted the relationship between substance abuse and individuals' selves and social identities changes, and how selves and social identities develop and transform during participants' addiction and recovery processes. Also overviewed were the particular methodswhich directed this study to an investigation of men's social processes of addiction and recovery. The focus of the analysis grew out of the issues and meanings that men attributed to self-changes in such processes. In the following chapter I consider the findings from this research which explore the preaddiction experiences of each participant.

3
Preaddiction Experiences

I didn't want to do nothing except smoke weed – not go to school. And that affected me quite a bit – got expelled for ten days and that was just like a vacation. I really wasn't worried about my education, I just wanted to party and have fun. I got my first DWI – I was 15 years old. (Travis)

The previous chapter provided a review of the theoretical and empirical research that highlighted the research question concerning the relationship between substance abuse and individuals' selves and social identities changes, along with how selves and social identities develop and transform during participants' addiction and recovery processes. Also overviewed was a summary of the methods that frames this study; that is, the qualitative approach linked with symbolic interactionism. In this chapter, I present the findings of this research through highlighting participants' preaddiction experiences similar to Travis' account above which include an overview of their lives before they became addicted.

The patterns of individual use, the social meanings ascribed to controlled substances, the approaches one takes to recovery, and emergent identities are mediated by the larger social context in which individuals are embedded (Granfield and Cloud 1999). Drug use/abuse can arise out of peer and familial relations, and can also be mediated by social class and cultural norms. Social structure provides the rules and resources involved in human action, both enabling and constraining individuals to act in certain ways (Giddens 1984). Our social actions and interactions are constrained by, yet generative of, the structural dimensions of social reality (Cohen 1987). Overall, the structural location of a person in society, including family environments, mediates their use/abuse of controlled substances. One of the participants, Rock, illustrates this argument as he states, "I come from a family of five and all five of us were drug addicts."

In this study, there is the opportunity to explore the major factors that impact on participants' lives as they begin to experiment with drugs and/or alcohol. It is also possible to explore how participants explain how individual and social selves come about, that is, how they make meanings of themselves in these various stages through influential factors that they consider important in their lives. This chapter presents two relevant themes: (1) a close analysis of how men's views of themselves emerge, along with the variegated problems they experience before they begin addictive careers in earnest; and (2) their significant experiences as they fully emerged into addiction.

In order to provide an overview for the men's stories, the following themes are highlighted in the following discussion: participants' family backgrounds; those men who experienced physical and/or sexual violence in their early years; participants' reasons for using and the extent of their drug and/or alcohol use. The men's personal views of how one becomes addicted along with an overview of the drugs they used in their early addiction experiences are also offered. Following this overview, their drugs of choice are summarized including how long they were addicted coupled with the ages of their full immersion into addiction. Also offered are highlights that relate to the fun and pleasure they experienced while within the drug and/or alcohol culture. For some of the men, prison and/or jail were events that they narrated as they became immersed into their use of substances. Finally, how the men managed their addiction, their thoughts about how they began to think about change and the elements of the beginning of such changes are highlighted.

Experimenting with Drugs and/or Alcohol

> In high school I was a very good baseball player. I didn't make it to the majors yet, but I was a pitcher and I was a second baseman and then that dream got away from me, you know. (Nick)

In the above quote, Nick is talking about his descent into drug use and how his use obliterated his dream of playing baseball. He continued by stating that he had been in contact with different scouts: "I was good, not tooting my own horn, but I was good." However, Nick explained further that he started hanging out with the wrong crowd, with the wrong people:

> I had a chance, I had a chance and I blew it. You know, when I see baseball teams now I should have been there. I was robbing and with people who were robbing. When I see the baseball teams now, I should have been there.

The goal of this section is to understand the basic social and social-psychological processes that depict participants' experiences as they experimented with substances. One of the significant questions in the interviews was what kind of lives participants had lived before they began to experiment with drugs and/or alcohol as highlighted by Nick's quote above. By listening to how these men perceived themselves as they preexperimented with drugs and/or alcohol, I came to a greater understanding of how they began their processes of using in the early phases of addiction.

I was interested in the answers to two questions regarding participants' preexperimental experiences: (1) who were these men before they became involved in the drug and/or alcohol culture, and (2) what were their lives like within their social environments during this time? The following discussion emphasizes participants' family backgrounds and their families' use of substances.

Men's Family Backgrounds

Family substance abuse was common among participants. As Table 3.1 shows 13 men had one to three family members who used drugs and/or alcohol to varying degrees, and 10 men had four or more family members who used. The remaining two participants grew up in families where drug and/or alcohol abuse was not an issue. Although some families used sporadically, such use was common in most participants' family environments. Family members were mothers, fathers, siblings, grandfathers,aunts and uncles. Many of their family members' addictions included various drugs, such as heroin and methamphetamines, but alcohol and marijuana, in many cases, were their families' drugs of choice.

Table 3.1. Addicted Family Members

Number of addicted family members	Frequency percent	(n)
0	8.0	(2)
1	12.0	(3)
2	32.0	(8)
3	8.0	(2)
4	16.0	(4)
5+	24.0	(6)
Total:	100.0	(25)

Participants' descriptions of themselves as they began to experiment with substances show that they oftentimes evaluate themselves in terms of how they are seen by their significant others, that is, by their families of origins as shown by the following quotes.

Herb's quote below mirrors many of the other participant's family's use of alcohol:

> Alcohol was everywhere, see, it was, to me, just a way of life, 'cause whatever we did, and wherever we went involving family, there was alcohol. All my cousins were drinking alcohol, if you have a barbecue, the first thing they do was get the alcohol, then figure out what we were gonna eat.

Several participants discussed their family use and how that affected them. For example, Travis grew up surrounded by alcohol abuse, but thought drinking was "cool": "You know Mum and Dad are doing it. Why can't I? I wanted to be like them." Further, Travis explained that he has two brothers, one half-brother and three half-sisters who use drugs:

> Every single one of them uses – except for one, my younger brother. I mean my brother; he was real big on the meth. Well both – all three of my brothers are. My younger brother and my younger sister, they're twins – they just turned 16. And it's been – they just want everything – anyway they can party.

His uncle was also using substances. "My uncle, he was really bad into the dope. You know, he'd do whatever it took so he could get some; he was in pretty bad shape."

Four participants discussed the fact that some family members with substance abuse problems were in fact dying because of their addictions. Rock described how his father was a heroin addict and his mother was an alcoholic. He continued by saying that a brother had in fact died from addiction.

Trent talked about his parents using marijuana quite heavily "up until you know, they had a family coming along and they stopped." He explains that his brother uses marijuana quite frequently but has seemed to stay away from other substances:

> I'm pretty sure that him seeing my experience with powders has completely kept him away from those, so ... I have to take one for the team like that to save my brother from the same kind of mistakes.

Herb stated that his parents and siblings also drank regularly:

My mother drank; my father drank for quite awhile, but then he just stopped, you know, he just said he wasn't gonna drink anymore, 'cause all of my father's siblings were dying from cirrhosis of the liver, they were drinking themselves to death.

Another participant, Daved, also explained that several members of his immediate family used as well as his close friends:

Uh, it was like my little brothers were doing it and I tried it and actually the first time I drank it I got sick, and said I would never do it again and that wasn't the case, I started drinking because my friend did it and it got to where I just had to have it, have it all the time, the whole time I was awake, even at work.

His father would also drink a six-pack of beer every night until he was in his early 60s. He continued by saying that "almost all of my uncles, and my grandfather did."

Oreste also explained that several members of his family used substances. "I am the oldest of four … two sisters younger than myself and then my brother. They all drank." He also described two of his great uncles as "bona fide alcoholics." For Oliver, both his parents were alcoholics.

Aaron's brother and adoptive family were also users:

Um, my real brother, yes, um, from what I can gather, I wasn't with him, when we got separated when we were getting adopted, he was sent to New York, I was in Chicago, um, from later on, whenever I visited him in federal prison he said that he did abuse drugs quite a bit and we did have the same drug of choice, which was meth. And my adoptive uncle and aunt, my adopted uncle is now in federal prison, for, he got 60 years for manufacturing, um, crystal meth, um, my adoptive aunt is in rehab for heroin. I have two adoptive cousins who are now in rehab.

One participant, David, explained that all of his brothers were alcoholics, as well as all of his uncles on his father's side: "All my brothers were alcoholics, they all quit and been clean for years, I was the last one left, as far as being clean." Duane explained that his father has been 13 years sober. Duane also has a sister who used to be an IV meth user. Although she still drinks, she does not use meth anymore.

JT explained that his mother had told him that his biological father was an alcoholic. But none of his immediate family members were involved in substance use. His sister "was the basketball star in the family growing up, she was the athletic type, you know." His brother was the only family member to use and only used marijuana recreationally.

Bobo explained that some of his family members used drugs and/or alcohol. He went on to discuss that his mother,

> Kinda smoked weed and drank during her pregnancy but she almost lost me, and … she stopped after I was born and she ain't used since.

Nick described his mother as someone who drank but explained she had stopped drinking once she got into her late 50s. Nick went on to say that all of his siblings were still active alcoholics; some of them were also using crack cocaine. His daughter who is 21 is in prison for sale of crack cocaine. Nick also noted that her mother, who is Nick's girlfriend, "is smoking crack right now."

Gorilla explained that his mother was an alcoholic. She left his real father for another man who was also an alcoholic. He said that both sides of his family were "all drinkers." D also described the majority of his family members as alcoholics. His mother did not use and "my dad's been in recovery for many, many years." However, his uncle and grandfather were also alcoholics.

Leonard stated that his father used marijuana and his stepmother used recreationally. Harvey explained that few members of his family used substances. However, his brother used methamphetamines while suffering from diabetes.

Sherman talked about his family and said that none of his siblings used. However, he described his mother and father as addicts and explained that when he was 16 years old, his mom passed away as a result of her addiction.

Another participant, Bishop, described his grandfather as an alcoholic. He also explained, "I had friends who had alcoholic families that I would hang out with." Timex also stated that his brother and his wife used to drink regularly as well:

> After work they would come home and drink. One day they discussed that if one wasn't going to buy it then the other wasn't going to drink it and they just stopped drinking. However, they are still smoking marijuana.

Further, Kid described both his uncles and both his grandfathers as alcoholics. Yet, he noted that his parents did not drink alcohol and did not allow it in their home. Kid explained that when growing up none of his immediate family members were drinkers. However, his first wife and children use:

> My first wife, to this day is … is an alcoholic, my brother-in-law. My son has started out with a lot of traits that I had, that I remember back – I wished he wouldn't have, but seems to be, I'm sure he's an alcoholic. My second son, he's 20 now –been drinking since he was probably 15, 16. His mother drinks on a daily basis, but she's a functional alcoholic, as they call it…you know, she works every day, comes home and drinks every night.

Martin stated that his aunt and uncle at one time both used alcohol. He also highlighted the fact that both his grandfathers had died due to an alcohol addiction: "One of them had a stroke because of his alcoholism and, uh, a couple days later died in the hospital. The other one just all kind of, like his body just basically shut down."

Aaron was a participant who had been born in Russia and adopted by a family:

> My real family we were in Russia, poor, you know, there's no drugs. My adoptive mom, she abused pills. My mom, she got into the military … she hurt herself somehow after she got out, so she was addicted to painkillers. I don't think I've ever seen her sober in my life. Still today.

Aaron continued his story about his adoptive family and his beginning use of alcohol:

> It was so, how can I say, it was so easy to come by, and alcohol was the first easy thing, cuz my adoptive dad, he's an alcoholic, so there's always alcohol in the house. Then at school once my friends found that I was drinking alcohol it was like, hey man, hit this, it was you know, marijuana, so I smoked a joint. And you know, it's basically alcohol was the gateway drug as we call it in rehab, the gateway drug, that led to everything else, which like I said, I made a mental note that I'm gonna try everything.

Two participants made note of that fact there was no substance abuse in their immediate families. For example, Blake explained that he was an only child and his parents never abused drugs and/or alcohol. "My parents … drank wine on Christmas, or, you know, with the family for a Christmas gathering. I'm almost 35; I've seen my parents drink once." And Sterling also explained that few of his immediate family members used substances. However, he described his grandparents and great-grandparents as alcoholics who drank well into their 80s and 90s.

When asked if anyone had influenced their use or abuse of controlled substances, a majority of the men discussed how the fact that individuals in their families were using impacted their own drug/alcohol use. A few of the men talked about substance use as such an integral part of their lives. If they did not use, it would be seen as almost "abnormal." As Rock explained,

> I think environment, peer pressure plays a big part, grow up in major cities and been exposed to this whole thing every day, you know … being exposed to alcohol at an early age, growing up, substance use was a normal part of everyday life.

Similar to other research (Baer and Corrado 1974; Chassin, Curran, Hussong and Colder 1996; Nurco, Kinlock, O'Grady and Hanlon 1998), the men's quotes as highlighted above show in most cases that the intimate environment of their family, that is, their families' excessive use of alcohol and/or drugs influenced them in their experimentation of substances.

This section has provided an overview of participants' families and the fact that in some way or another, they had been influenced by their family use and abuse of substances. The following section discusses those men who had experienced some type of physical or sexual abuse and the impact such abuse had on their lives.

Men Who Experienced Physical and/or Sexual Violence

Several research studies have considered high rates of childhood physical and sexual victimization among alcohol and/or drug-dependent men. (Blood and Cornwall 1996; Chassin et al. 1996; Clark et al. 2001; Fergusson, Boden, and Horwood 2008; Fiorentine et al. 1999; Gil-Rivas et al. 1997; Liebschutz et al. 2002; Pirard et al. 2005). Springer, Sheridan, Kuo and Carnes (2007) argue that childhood maltreatment has been associated with an array of psychological and somatic symptoms in adult life. Blood and Cornwall (1996) found that 62 percent of men who reported sexual abuse also reported physical abuse, compared to 32 percent of those who reported no sexual abuse. They also found that sexually abused adolescents reported an earlier onset of alcohol and other drug use than did nonabused adolescents. Five participants in this study also experienced such abuse.

For example, Oliver had his first experience with alcohol at a young age. His earliest recollection was around the age of eight years old: "When the old man wanted a beer he'd give me the bottle with so much in it, and I would get that as a reward for fetching one." He also explained that his father used to be physically abusive toward him and often his father would "send him to the barn." This meant that his father would eventually come out to beat him. Oliver began hiding alcohol in the barn and learned that drinking prior to a beating would help lessen the pain. He continued his explanation:

> I mean he was, he'd drink a few beers and after he got home from work or something and then he'd get around to his business and he'd tell me go to the barn. I knew what it meant so I, I knew he'd be a few minutes before he got there, he liked to make me sweat, and think about what was gonna happen.

Interestingly, D had also suffered physical abuse at the hands of his grandfather but does not attribute those experiences to his addiction: "I'd rather accept responsibility for my own actions."

Leonard also suffered abuse from his parents, especially from his dad:

> There was definitely physical abuse, there was definitely ... verbal, mental, yeah my father was real heavy ... the, he probably said to me ... a thousand times, "You no good, rotten schmuck!"

There were two other men who also discussed abuse in their early years. Gorilla explained that his stepfather was physically abusive toward him and his brothers. In continuing his story, he talks about one of his brothers who also abused him: "My oldest brother, he, his abuse was different; he would just look at me like everything I said was just stupid." He also discussed instances of sexual abuse in which his brother "you know; he would touch me in places where he shouldn't."

Duane talked about a man who lived not far from him, who had a black belt in karate. He liked to teach people karate and show them how to make arrowheads: "He had all of the stuff that attracted young boys, he was a pedophile and he used drugs ... two and a half years that guy you know, molested me, but he gave me drugs, which I was just scared to tell anybody about that."

The following section highlights men's experimentation with drugs and/or alcohol and how and why they began to experiment.

Reasons for Using

> I loved it. Changed my life, right then. Before I drank I was just a
> scared nervous little kid, but it did something for me, and it changed
> my view of myself and everyone else, almost instantaneously. (Duane)

Participants' introduction to substances was initiated through various influences: families, friends, and for two participants, it was for post-surgical pain. The contexts of drugs and/or alcohol experimentation for most of the men (n=22) consisted of social groups with peers and/or family. The following table highlights the men's reasons for experimenting.

Table 3.2. Reasons for Experimenting with Alcohol and/or Drugs

Reasons	Frequency percent	(n)
Used with family	36	(9)
Used with friends	52	(13)
Other	12	(3)
Total:	100	(25)

Nine participants had their first experiences at an early age with their family members, 13 used with friends and three for other reasons, for example, post-surgery pain and to deal with emotional problems. For example, Gorilla explained that he began drinking occasionally when he was only a young boy at the age of eight: "It wasn't that a big a deal, parents didn't really care." He explained that he did not use alcohol consistently until the age of 16. In fact, growing up he said he despised alcohol, the way people smelled when they drank it and the inconsistencies and behaviors that followed as he further stated:

> I hated everything about it, you know, didn't have a lot of money for
> food, school clothes or anything, yet, there was money for alcohol and
> a refrigerator full of beer.

Another participant, D, began sneaking his father's alcohol at the age of eight. He said that his father was an alcoholic and often left alcohol lying around: "I'd find it, see my dad drink it … and go grab one of his beers and sneak off with it, so it wasn't really that big of a deal." D highlighted his initial experience when he first became intoxicated:

The first time I actually remember using was, my dad grounding me in seventh grade … I ran away for a week and a half. My brother lived in the same area, so that night I went to a party at his friend's house. The first weekend I kissed a girl, was the first weekend I had sex, was the first weekend I remember getting drunk, was the first time I tripped acid, was the first time I tried coke, was the first time I smoked marijuana.

D expanded on why he used:

Well, I wasn't really, yeah, I mean, I would find it and drink it, it wasn't like I was getting drunk, you know what I mean? I'd find it, see my dad drink it, put it away and go grab one of his beers and sneak off with it, so it wasn't really that big of a deal. Then, my mom and dad split up, I went to live with my grandpa, and it was one of [his] big deals with him, you know, if you're on his … knuckle team, then you got to drink a Jack and Coke like he drank, and that was when I was like fifth grade, sixth grade.

Sherman first started sneaking beer when he was around nine years old. He explained that when his parents would have parties, he and his cousins would sneak alcohol. The first time he ever smoked marijuana was at the age of 11. And, too, he explained that:

The first time I smoked marijuana was with my ma, me and my sister. It was actually right in front of our home … she told me and my sister that she would prefer us if we ever do try drugs or whatever to do them at home instead of in the streets.

Oreste first tasted alcohol at the age of eight when he sneaked some alcohol from his father's liquor cabinet. Oreste also explained that when he was in grade school his father had begun to make his own homemade wine. When the kids at school became aware of this they began to threaten Oreste with physical violence. They promised that they would not beat him up if he stole some wine from his father and brought it to school. At the age of 11 he was at a friend's house with a few other friends. He explained:

They were mixing everything their parents had possible into a tumbler and they were passing it around. I walked home about half a mile. I walked in the door and my mother looked at me and said, "You're drunk, I'm not gonna bother even talking to you or disciplining you until you can feel it in the morning and you have your headache."

Although Oreste had experienced alcohol at a young age he was not using consistently. He did not drink again until he was in college where he got drunk several times, and, as he explained, "[I was] drunk to the point of losing the ability to walk or steady myself."

Martin talked about first tasting alcohol when he was in the third grade but did not use again until he was in seventh grade. It was in the eighth grade he explained, that he had begun to drink heavily. Martin also stated that he first started using marijuana because of his older sister.

Another participant, Duane, explained how he began drinking the day he finished the sixth grade. He and a friend had brought a bottle of vodka to a graduation party and put it in the punch. Duane described his first experience with alcohol as a positive one. He explained that the alcohol gave him the confidence that he had never had before.

Herb related his story of his initial use:

> I drank this beer and I thought it was the most awful beverage I ever put in my mouth, disgusting. But at 13, I was at the stage where I was trying to fit in. So the fellas got some tall cans of Ol' English malt liquor, and I drank, I guess about three cans of that, and came home and threw up all over the place and drunk and the guys had to carry me downstairs, 'cause I stayed in the basement of the house. That's where it started. I was 13, they was 15, 16, but I wanted to hang out with the group, the cool group, and, I guess that was kind of, I ain't gonna say initiation, but if you gonna hang out, you gonna get, you gonna drink.

Travis said that he started sneaking alcohol at the age of 12. He explained that both his mother and father were alcoholics. Growing up his parents separated and his mother developed relationships with other men. However, Travis explained that they were also alcoholics and drug addicts. He talked about how he would have his friends come over and drink:

> My mum was getting into trouble because my friends were getting drunk and then having to go home. My friends' parents actually paid attention to their kids – my mum didn't care. She was worried about running out of alcohol.

Interestingly, Travis' mother was also the first to introduce him to marijuana. He further elaborated on his initial use:

> I first started using because I'd sit around watch my mum and I always wanted to sit in the living room while they were sitting there getting high. Finally my mum said, "Here, try it, if you think you're man

enough to do it – here, go ahead and try it." Smoked the first time, fell in love. About two weeks later my mum started having me sell her drugs for her.

Leonard first got drunk at an early age:

> I first started using alcohol. I remember drinking hard cider as a youth, I guess … but … that was, all I got out of that was just a little warm fuzzy feeling … then was I was probably 11 … I drank probably a shot of whiskey … and I got a little more than a warm fuzzy feeling but that was about it … when I was 13 … I drank a little whiskey at school and that summer, I started … that summer I got drunk, and, well actually I may have been 12 … the summer that I was 12, I got drunk, my mother had a party, and the night before and I took a hit off of every bottle there was in the liquor cabinet.

Leonard goes on to say that within six months all of his barriers were down. He began using and experimenting with the many different substances that were popular at the time and by the time he was 16, he was also drinking every day.

Bishop talked about how he began using both alcohol and other substances before the age of 12. However, he explained that he did not develop an addiction until he was about 17 when he began using both heroin and cocaine:

> How it came about is I always say I think it had a lot to do with my family structure, which was very intact and a very Christian-based home. I didn't have any brothers, only had one sister and so I sought that brother relationship with people outside my home and a lot of those in the area that I grew up were a negative influence, I wanted to be liked, I wanted to be accepted, peer pressure that kind of thing, I had some low self-esteem.

Sterling began using alcohol at the age of 13. He explained that he and his friend would pick up discarded bottles of alcohol and drink them:

> I used to pick it up off the side of the road, a lot of teenagers lived on my street and they would just throw it out on the curb at night I guess when they went home; I pick it up the next day and drink it.

Another participant, Buck, also began using alcohol at the age of 13. When asked where he got the money to buy the alcohol he said that it was easily accessible. Buck elaborated:

> My parents were alcoholics, and my grandparents, and I just shared
> with them. My whole family is alcoholics, grandfather died from it,
> my mother and father both died from it, and my grandmother she
> didn't die from it, she was a bad alcoholic too.

Sherman explained that he had become involved with gangs at the
very young age of 10 or 11 years old. He grew up in a very poor
neighborhood where there was also a lot of homelessness. Sherman
noted that while he was in the gang "as far as the actual robbery and
stuff like that, I never was off into nothing like that ... what I mostly did
was the drug selling."

Participants were not using consistently at the time. Their
experimentation and use developed from their initial experiences. The
majority of participants discussed the fact that immediate family
members were users themselves, thus making drugs and/or alcohol
easily accessible. Some participants' family members were not upset by
the fact that their children had their first experiences with substances at
such an early age. Some family members even encouraged such
behavior. This type of socialization may have shaped participants' views
and feelings toward certain substances.

Participants explained that witnessing the behavior over time led
them to become comfortable with certain substances and their use. Such
an explanation mirrors studies that have concentrated on the intimate
environment of family influences as excessive use of drugs and/or
alcohol on the part of the parents have been found to influence male
children in experimenting with and continuing addictive behaviors (Baer
and Corrado 1974; Chassin et al. 1996; Nurco et al.1998).

Several participants' experiences were with their school friends. For
example, Nick's first experience with marijuana was with such a group
of friends in school. He said,

> I wanted to be cool with other fellows. I was always kind of influenced
> by seeing [them] do it and seen friends do it, so I thought it would be
> the right thing to do.

Another participant, Kid, began using alcohol at the age of 15. He
remembers clearly how he began to drink:

> It was Wild Turkey 101, I remember, and ... why ... I just started high
> school it was early, like the first month of high school, we was outside
> sitting before school started in the parking lot, one of the older, like a
> junior or senior, pulled out a half pint of Wild Turkey, and it was two
> of us guys sitting around, he said, I got a 20 dollar bill here if anybody

thinks they can down this without stopping. Well, I was sure somebody was gonna say something, and I never drank, but I knew I could drink a pint of anything, you know, and put 20 bucks down was alright for me back then, so, so I did and I did! And ... to make a long story short, my mom was coming to get me at second hour, when my shop teacher took me up to the principal's office for drinking, and I got to go home free from school that day. I was pretty intoxicated.

Timex also explained that he first used alcohol in high school like most others did. He said that he had been raised around alcohol and enjoyed the taste of beer and "by the time I was 21, it was a daily trip to the beer store." Rock explained how his experimentation began at age 16 due to his best friend's use: "What made me really start shooting heroin was one of my best friends, he was selling it."

Blake also began his experience with drugs in high school. He smoked marijuana but did not enjoy the effects of it and did not use regularly. He also experimented with mushrooms. He and some friends had mixed the mushrooms into a milkshake using a blender. Blake explained it as just one of those things he did "'cause everyone else did it."

McIntosh and McKeganey (2002) suggest that the main reasons for participants' initial drug use were not only curiosity but also a desire to comply with the expectations of others, especially peers; a strong predictor of adolescent drug use is the extent to which one associates with other adolescents who use drugs (Bahr et al. 1995; Elliott, Huizinga and Ageton 1985).

Much of the literature argues that problem drug use appears most prevalent during a developmental period of "emerging adulthood," whichextends from 16 to 25 years of age (Sussman, Skaraand Ames 2008).Substancesof all types are being widely used or misused by teens and emerging adults inthe United States (as cited in Sussman et al. 2008; Johnson, Listwan, Sundt, Holsinger and Latessa 2003). Researchers and practitioners have arguedthat some substance use represents normal development among teens or may be viewedas part of normal development by their peers, as they begin to explore different life roles (Sussman et al. 2008).

Rock explained how his experimentation with different drugs and alcohol led to harder substances:

First thing that I used was probably alcohol, then marijuana, then I started dropping pills and then drinking Robitussin and by the age of 16, I was shooting heroin.

He explained that he was not particularly fond of marijuana and thus there was a reason for him to "advance" to another drug. He said that he first started using heroin because one of his best friends was selling it:

> What made me really start shooting heroin was one of my best friends, he was selling it. We was in the house and he was helping himself to drugs. Guys would be coming to his house, men and women – all the time, day and night.

Rock went on to say that it was ironic that he had become a heroin addict. He explained that when he was in school he was very afraid of needles. On many occasions, when students had to get shots he would come home from school crying. The reason he began using heroin was because of his curiosity and the accessibility of the drug:

> I remember the first day when we was up in his house and they had just got through shooting up and I was just looking at them, and it looked like they was feeling good. This one particular day I decided to say, okay, I'd go ahead and try it.

Daved also said that his first experience with marijuana was with a group of friends. He said that he got marijuana from "a friend at work…. I said sure, I'd love to try it." He goes on to describe his first experience as an unpleasant one as he became confused and disoriented with his surroundings. He explained that he did not want to smoke marijuana again. However:

> [T]wo or three weeks later, some guys from _____; they said come to their party. The first thing I saw was a glass, there was about 20-something joints in it … I started smoking some of it, and we smoked all those joints and just had a ball, and then, from then on, as far as I was concerned, marijuana was it.

Trent explained that at the age of 18, once he had graduated from high school, he began living with one of his friends. His friend was living with a drug dealer and had begun using methamphetamines. Trent continued saying that he had never used methamphetamines before, but as he was constantly in close contact with the drug and people who used, he became more comfortable:

> So we started hanging around there too much and basically [I] just got really curious and then comfortable with it, I guess comfortable seeing it, and [I] started doing it.

Three participants began using due to other factors in their lives: two for post-surgery help with their pain and one due to an emotional event in his life. Blake had begun using painkillers after he had kidney surgery. "I was put on painkillers because of that. After my prescription ran out, and the pain was still there, I had to find a new way to deal with the pain."

Oreste talked about how he was involved in a terrible car accident with a snowplow, in which the snowplow tore off the roof of the vehicle and a part of the roof collapsed onto his head. He was put on life support and suffered irreversible brain damage. Oreste explained that after his accident he "started having severe problems sleeping, as a result of the head trauma, and I began to self-medicate."

One participant, D, described a terrible event in his life that influenced his substance use. This event occurred when his baby girl died: "That's when I started heroin, because it made it all go away."

Although the majority of participants had their first experiences with drugs and/or alcohol at an early age, there is one participant who did not use until the age of about 24. JT stated that the reason for his initial experience with methamphetamines was that he "ran into the wrong crowd" as he began using with his friends. He became involved with an individual who would steal car stereos and sell them to make money to buy the drugs. JT's friend was eventually caught and sent to prison. At this time JT explained that he was able to stay away from the methamphetamines for a period of time. Yet, when he met others who were using he would find himself using methamphetamines again. He continued to say: "I didn't know what I was dealing with. There's a big crowd out there of people that do it."

This section has provided an overview of the reasons for participants' experimentation with substances. The following discussion highlights the extent of their drug and/or alcohol use and their resultant experiences.

Extent of Drugs and/or Alcohol Use

When asked the extent of their drugs and/or alcohol use, the majority of participants described excessive use. Three participants explained that they would drink alcohol until they fell into unconsciousness. They also noted that they felt unable to control themselves, and once they began to drink they were unable to stop. When asked the extent of his drug use Kid responded:

I was getting to the point where I couldn't go out and drink without blackin' out ... the time I graduated high school, you know, when I graduated high school I would stop and get me a 12-pack, 'cause I thought "well I worked, I worked all day; I'm entitled to a beer." Well, didn't take long to lead up to 12 beers a day ... I would black out every night and I couldn't control it, I couldn't stop, and I wouldn't stop until I blacked out.

Bobo also stated: "I drank until I go to sleep, or pass out ... I start off with beer, and then go to gin, or whiskey at night time or, but just all out through the day." Herb mentioned:

Well as far as the cocaine, oh, I could say, a quarter ounce a week easy, and, uh, the alcohol, a couple of fifths of whiskey. Once I popped the top that's it, see I learned, I didn't know how to drink, I knew how to get drunk. I envy people who can pop a refreshing cold beer, yeah, sit down have one or two and just relax ... but I don't know how to stop right there.

Three participants noted that when they first began using drugs and/or alcohol, they did not use very large amounts. However, as their use continued, they developed a tolerance to such substances. As a result, they needed to use larger quantities in order to achieve the high they wanted. Travis noted: "Usually it only takes a little bit, but for me, I'd done it for so long ... that it would take that much for me. I'd probably do a gram of crystal meth ... a day."

Daved also stated:

The wine, within a period of a year, year and a half, it, my, um, tolerance built up so that it would, one bottle wasn't enough, so then I had to have two bottles, and that wasn't enough, so I would buy the third bottle.

Trent also talked about a different way in which to use substances in order to achieve a better high:

Me and my friend, that first summer, me and him would just sniff it [methamphetamines] and I couldn't really tell ya how much I used then. Once you get a tolerance by taking it through your nose, you look for the next step up to try to get back to that initial feeling you know, so then I started shooting.

Trent continued his story:

I was living with the people that got it at price you know, so, we weren't really having to pay for that much of it, and what we did, we got a lot more than what we paid for, and it was just, it was just there, the whole time, I mean, you'd get spun or whatever and do whatever you did, and as soon as you came down there, there it was again … we weren't in the situation where we got cracked out and then started coming down and had to run around town for days or whatever looking for more, it was like you turned around and there it was still.

When asked the extent of his drug use, Bishop said that at times he would use five or six hundred dollars a day worth of heroin. Bishop noted that he had to steal in order to support his habit: "I either made enough or went to jail trying to get it." He went on to say that his drug use consumed his everyday life:

You have to understand that this is a 24 hour job which means that a lot of times when other people were trying to get home, eat dinner and rest, I was concentrating on my next hustle so that I would have a fix in the morning when I woke up.

Duane stated that he "bought probably an eight ball of meth a day." To support his habit, Duane had to steal money from his great-grandmother. Duane mentioned that stealing made him feel terrible:

I have to do something even worse so I can get the money to get the dope so I can—and it's just a terrible, terrible cycle and by the end of it, I can't seem to do enough dope to make me feel okay.

Another participant, Sterling, almost died due to the level of his alcohol use. He stated that: "Through high school everybody knew I always had a fifth behind my seat, and I was drinking about a fifth a day. It was gonna kill me if I didn't stop." Sterling discussed a time whereby he overdosed on methamphetamines: "I was clinically dead for 82 seconds; they said, um, if I ever drank again it could kill me."

Other participants also described using large quantities of drugs and/or alcohol. Oliver stated that he drank whiskey and usually drank: "A couple fifths a day. I could drink and drink and drink and drink … drank it like it was water."

D was addicted to methamphetamines and noted that he used "half a gram to a gram … yeah per day. There's nothing like the feeling of taking a quarter gram of pure crystal meth, and putting it into your blood stream."Along with using methamphetamines, D said that "Some days I'd go to the bar and I'd drink … probably have 12, 15 beers."

Another participant, David, also used large quantities of methamphetamines as he stated:

> Most of the times I came home and sleep but most of the time you can't and end up staying up the whole day and then have to work that night, and I did that for a while, then it caught up and drove my body down … sometimes you go seven, eight, nine days with no sleep at all. Then you start seeing, I mean you start hearing things.

There were three participants who talked about using drugs in moderate amounts. Gorilla noted that he used methamphetamines on weekends or socially with others. JT noted that he used "just a little bit here and there and maybe on the weekends and that was pretty much it." Martin also used moderate amounts of marijuana – he only used about six times a week.

Several men also talked about developing a tolerance to certain substances, where their drug and/or alcohol use only increased in order to attain their initial high. The great majority also had their addictions and habits consume their everyday lives. Several men talked about using excessively to the point of unconsciousness. They noted that once they began using a particular substance they felt unable to control themselves.

Overall, many of the men described their initial experiences as taking place with friends or family members. Some participants had first started using drugs and/or alcohol because others were doing it and they wanted to be a part of the group. For some men, having family members use such substances may have led them to view such behavior as normative. For others, difficult times in their lives influenced their decisions to use particular substances. Lower family bonds and drug or alcohol abusing family members increases the likelihood of an adolescent associating with peers who drink or use drugs. Nurco et al. (1998) argue that children with deviant parents and those who lack a close relationship with nondeviant parents were more likely than other children to associate with deviant peers and to be vulnerable to peers' influences, similar to participants' experiences.

Personal Views of How One Becomes Addicted

How does one become addicted? Much of the literature offers various answers to this question (Anderson 1991; Becker 1953; Denzin 1987a/b; Haas 2003; Kiecolt 1994; McIntosh and McKeganey 2002; Peele 1989; Taber 1993). For example, Becker's (1953) early work on marijuana use helps us to understand that drug experimentation provides meaning to the user as he argues that:

> [It is] a sequence of social experiences during which the person acquires a conception of the meaning of the behavior, and perceptions and judgments of objects and situations, all of which make the activity possible and desirable. (p. 235)

Denzin (1987a, p. 51) further argues;

> A theory of addiction cannot explain addiction solely in terms of the effects that the drug in question produces for the user. Not only are such explanations tautological, and hence untestable, but they fail to locate the key factor in addiction, which is the user's symbolic and interactional relationship with the drug. The self of the user lies at the core of the addiction process.

In addition to looking at the addicts' initiation into alcohol and drug use, McIntosh and McKeganey (2002) examined the progression into abuse and dependence: an unconscious "drift" rather than as a result of a deliberate decision; the influence of relationships or peer groups who provided opportunity and encouragement to use more regularly; boredom resulting from unemployment or poor recreational activities; to cope with life problems and escape from reality; or to overcome feelings of personal inadequacy, such as shyness or lack of confidence.

Peele (1989) contends that people become involved in addictive experiences as they need a sense of power and control and to create satisfactory self-esteem. Individuals become addicted due to varying factors: social and cultural forces include social class, peer and parental influences, culture, ethnicity, stress, social support, intimacy, and positive rewards. Individual factors may include choice of the addictive object, lack of values and self-restraint, health, antisocial attitudes, intolerance, uncertainty, belief in magical solutions, low self-esteem, lack of self-efficacy and external loss of control.

Denzin (1987a) Haas (2003) and Anderson (1991) indicate that an altered sense of identity or a dissociative-like state occurs in an individual's life that predisposes them to addiction. Denzin (1987a, p. 21) further argues that the addicted individual (self) uses drugs to escape an "inner emptiness of self." This emptiness can be manifested in a fundamental instability of self-experience. The individual seeks transcendence from how they see their reality, and addiction becomes the "fix" for the emotional pain (Haas 2003, p. 36). Therefore, it can be argued that addiction is used as a crutch; as a means of finding a valued self-feeling that will transcend the inner lack that is felt on a regular basis. In other words, drugs are used as an anesthetic to escape from deep problematics of the self as the individual becomes fixated on the ritual and object of their addiction (Haas 2003, Denzin 1987a).

A sense of a hated self is also believed to develop in addiction processes (Anderson 1991; Denzin 1987a; Haas 2003). In these studies, the self of the user lies at the core of the addiction process, thus, addiction may be understood as one's avoidance of intimacy with a hated self (Peele 1989).

Haas (2003) argues that most addicts retrospectively interpret their childhoods as difficult, where they felt like they "didn't belong" or they were "different." In this case, addiction can be seen as a dependent state acquired over time by an individual in their attempt to relieve such chronic stresses or strain conditions (Kiecolt 1994; Haas 2003). Such childhood experiences that produce a deep sense of personal inadequacy and rejection can predispose an individual to addiction (Haas 2003; Taber 1993), due to ego identity discomfort and a felt loss of control in defining an identity (Anderson 1991).

Other authors (see Baer and Corrado 1974; Chassin et al. 1996; Nurco et al. 1998) argue that intimate environment of family influences, poor parenting; parental absence, separation, or divorce; family conflict; deviant behavior among family members; excessive use of alcohol and/or drugs on the part of the parents have been found to influence male children in experimenting with and continuing addictive behaviors, similar to the participants in this study. Overall, lower family bonds and drug or alcohol abusing family members increased the likelihood of an adolescent associating with peers who drink or use drugs (Bahr et al. 1995).

In addition, extant research suggests that a strong predictor of adolescent drug use is the extent to which one associates with other adolescents who use drugs (see Bahr et al. 1995; Elliott et al. 1985). McIntosh and McKeganey's (2002) findings suggest the main reasons for participants' initial drug use were curiosity and a desire to comply with the expectations of others, especially peers.

Similarly, other research studies (see Blood and Cornwall 1996; Chassin et al. 1996; Clark et al. 2001; Fiorentine et al. 1999; Gil-Rivas et al. 1997; Liebschutz et al. 2002; Pirard et al. 2005) suggest that high rates of childhood physical and sexual victimization are common among alcohol and/or drug-dependent men.

So *how* did the men I interviewed see this issue? Martin stated that for him addiction meant:

I would say the need or dependence on something just to, where you can't really function without it, uh, your body craved it physically and mentally.

Martin's quote was reiterated by many of the participants. Many participants' responses to my question involved their use with their families and significant others. For example, Bobo stated:

I think it's a lot of what you see as you growin' up. I honestly think that if you grow up seein' family members, mom and dad doin' drugs every day ... I think that you're gonna go out and do it. And once you try it, I mean, it's already in your head that it's okay because mom and daddy doin' it.

Bobo further expanded on how his friends influenced his use:

It wasn't only my parents, it was the peers outside, outside my household that ... I came from a small town, and everybody hung out in this one particular area and just, again, this goes back to just seein' it every day. And then, the same way that I thought it was a normal thing ... when you grow up you get a certain age you get to smoke weed and you get to drink and you can hang out with this person and that's the cycle that you end up fallin' into and then it's like an everyday routine.

Nick suggested that how one gets addicted has to do with friends who are using:

I believe that how you get addicted is being around it most of the time, having friends that have it, and you know, having it around. I mean plentiful, the liquor and everything, people that drink a lot, you have the situation right there with them, you know, and so, ah, and it starts and after like awhile you don't depend on them, you depend on yourself, you know.

Daved's definition was clear:

The definition of addiction: well, I think, you know, the person starts basing his entire life around his drinking, you know, people that overeat, or are addicted to sex or if there is anything where they start basing their life around it, you're addicted. You can't, you can't go a day or two, three days without it, without it causing problems of some type [then] you've got an addiction.

Daved also talked about becoming an addict as he stated: "The first time that I got drunk, that whiskey drunk, I knew right then and there I wanted to do that all the time." Daved also believed that there is a genetic component to addiction as he stated: "A lot of people think that the studies have shown that it can run through families and my family is a classic example of that."

David was another participant who believed his family's use as well as his peers played a role in his addiction: "I would most definitely say that running around with the wrong crowd, definitely being around it, or if your family members drink." David talked about how his addiction developed as he got older: "I became 16, then the more I try it ... I drunk two beers and I was sick for a few days and I said not me, and ... gradually I was out partying with all of the guys all of the time and then it got worse and worse." It quickly got to the point where "you gotta have it to function, if you don't, you don't get up and do nothing.

For others, it was curiosity. Rock noted that he began using:

By trying it – by curiosity. I wonder what this would feel like, I wonder what they feel like – that's how I got addicted. I would ask myself, "What are they getting out of this little-bitty pill," you know, because it's such a small pill so it was just basically curiosity.

As well, Rock enhanced his definition by stating that someone gets addicted because they are always chasing the feeling of their initial high:

That's what keeps the person on that journey because you think you can get it one more time, one more time and you can never get it again. Addiction to me is basically anything that would make me feel good. Anything that I enjoy I can get addicted to.

Sherman defined addiction as something that is strongly needed in someone's life:

Addiction, I, I define addiction as far as anything that what you need more than anything, not only drugs or alcohol. It could be work, it could be food, it could be a person, it could be sex or whatever. Um, addiction to me is anything that alters your mind from a "normal" state of being.

For Trent, addiction was a way of escaping his reality: "[I used] just to escape the unfun boring reality that is life, you know, and do something a little bit more fun. A lot of my drug use has come from, uh, it being an escape mechanism."

For Martin when he first started using he stated that:

> I was just experimenting and after a while experimentation turned, I really like it and I like that feeling so I want to have it more often. It happens so slowly, but at the same time so quickly, you know, 'cause you're, you're in the moment. I just couldn't get enough.

Martin continued to talk about his sister's use influencing his own decisions to use alcohol and/or drugs:

> My sister, uh we were close, even to this day we're close. She didn't have anything bad happen to her, all the rumors I had heard about using or whatever, she kinda disproved of them all, and because she was standing there in front of me telling me that she had done this ... and she liked it.

Not surprisingly, other participants enjoyed their use: Travis was using and continued because of "the enjoyment of it." When he first started doing meth, he stated, "Ah, marijuana, I loved it. I didn't like to come down, so I tried to stay up as long as I could."

Trent also offered his definition in an oblique way:

> I don't know how you can define it unless you put an addictive substance in front [of] person A, the addictive one, and [an] addictive substance in front of person B, the addictive one and see how they deal with them differently because I don't think you can really judge an addictive personality unless you give them some sort of temptation to be addicted to, you know.

There are some participants who believed that addiction to drugs and/or alcohol is a choice while others did not. JT stated that: "One does get addicted because they choose to." For JT, "It's definitely a choice. It was my choice to go back and get more and continue that lifestyle."

However, Daved was clear in his definition and strongly believes that addiction is not a choice but a disease:

> I've read so many things on so many people that find that they don't believe that drug addiction is disease and I know that it is, because I did not chose to become a worthless piece of crap, I didn't choose to become a drunken sot, you know, maybe in the history of alcoholism there are people that say, yeah, I want to become a worthless piece of shit, and so I will start drinking and this is what I want to become, that doesn't make any sense, that's a statement that so, that's like the insanity of the alcoholism itself, it's just pure ignorance though, people and I think that, um, there's a term in the AA called instant alcoholic,

without question, I was an instant addict, the first time that I got drunk, that whiskey drunk, I knew right then and there I wanted to do that all the time.

Interestingly, Bishop talked about genetic predisposition and how an individual's genetics may cause them to react differently to certain substances. Bishop also felt that there are individuals who have addictive personalities and one may become addicted to more than just drugs and alcohol:

Gambling, caffeine (coffee) but the difference between being addicted to coffee and being addicted to narcotics is that coffee doesn't usually cause you to lose control of your life. I guess you would have to put a personality on addiction. I think addiction does have its own personality but I also believe that two of the components of addiction are obsession and compulsion, okay, obsession of the mind, once you get that idea fixed in your head, you can't get it out until you use, compulsion is once you start using you can't stop it. So, I do believe there are people who suffer from compulsive and obsessive thinking patterns that cause them to do something over and over again that could lead to addiction if they put chemicals with it.

Bishop expanded on his definition:

Addiction is an individual who uses substances that eventually they lose control of part of or all of their lifestyle. An addict is an individual whose whole life is centered around getting drugs, alcohol or chemicals and see the difference a lot of people try and make a difference in that, because some people are responsible to a point, but an addict is a person who loses control over his responsibilities.

Further, Bishop reiterated a theoretical issue:

Well, figure this. Ah, for a family of four, three boys and a girl, one is an addict, one becomes a doctor, one becomes a lawyer, you know, grew up in the same environment, same family structure, but one of them becomes addicted. So, you know, it gets down to choices now, you know, the choices that I make, the things that I want to take responsibility for.

Sterling also felt that there are individuals with addictive personalities and that one can become addicted to anything, even "chocolate or whatever." He continued to state:

Um, I think addiction would just be when you feel like you're gonna go crazy without whatever it is that you're craving, that you can't get through each day without thinking about it and without it just bothering you, like I just wanna get high, I just wanna get high and doing crazy stupid things to get that, to achieve it, I think that would be addiction.

As well, D felt that he was predisposed to becoming an addict. He stated that he became addicted and was using "to get away." D also believed that some individuals may have addictive personalities: "I think some people; some people have the ability to become addicted and some people don't." He expanded on his views:

Umm, addiction to me? Addiction to me was, you know, shooting so much morphine that I had to do increased amounts of speed to stay up and staying up for 7, 8, 9 days at a time sometimes, and it was just how I lived, it was how I was. To me, I needed the drug, I needed it because it allowed me to stay up, because when I was up, I wasn't wasting time, because sleep is nothing but a waste of time, that's how I viewed it back then, and people that couldn't stay up as long as I could, they were weak, you know, they were weak, because they couldn't do as much drugs as I could. I think it's just when you need something in your life to feel normal. That's how I've defined it, and at the time, I needed that to feel normal, I needed it to feel good about myself, I didn't feel good unless I was on something, or had access to something, and it made me feel important.

Duane offered the following clarification:

I think if alcohol and drugs do something for you, if they alter your perception of reality, enough to make it okay to just breathe, then that's drug addiction. And, uh, I think you probably need to add a physical factor there, once you start you don't have any control over how much you're going to take.

Aaron articulated his explanation succinctly:

My definition, personal definition of addiction is when I cannot take any more stress or whatever the factor may be in my life, but I just can't take anymore and need a release. So you start looking for one, people's addictions can be food, you know, anything, so, it helps take you out of your frame of mind, it helped try to ease the pain of living, or maybe depression or anxiety or whatever it may be and, uh, it's what we abuse, what we use to abuse, basically, and I've always told my case worker, my counselor in rehab, drugs are not the problem, humans are the problem, we have the problem of abusing the drugs, the drugs don't abuse us, so, it's for whatever you want to, whatever your need is at that time or desire to help get you away from reality.

Timex stated that, for him, addiction meant that: "it is where you've got to have it, whether it be a drug or booze, you've got to have it, uh, you can't do without it; just to have it yeah, to know that I had it, you know."

For Oliver, addiction was about being out of control:

Well addiction to me is, is when you're doing something that you don't want to do, but you don't have control of it, you, your, it's outta, it's outta your conscious control, uh, something that you don't understand drives you to do what you are addicted to, whether it's drugs or alcohol, or sex, or porn, whatever. You know, uh, and um, I don't think I was addicted as a child, I was addicted to curiosity maybe, trying to figure out what the hell's going on, uh, but it, it's uh, it's something that seems to have a lot of control over you without you being able to do much about it because—and there again, it's simply information, understanding, I believe, uh, and um.

For Blake, addiction was a desperate situation:

Addiction is, wow, to me addiction just is, is, is, basically, I couldn't go through the day without having the drugs, or I couldn't, I couldn't function at all without it, zip, zero, zilch, I couldn't do anything. And there were times where I would go, you know, 5 or 6 days without having anything because I didn't have the money at the time, or I couldn't steal the money, and I didn't have the money, and I would go 5 or 6 days, and it was just, that's all I could think about, you know, how soon is the money gonna get here so I can get some more pills.

For Leonard, his use was connected to his lack of self-esteem as a young man. His use of drugs empowered him as he stated:

You know, I love feeling an empowered feeling ... they ... you know, if I did some ... downs and some speed ... which would be like ... cheap speed ball ... they ... which I never did heroin, I've just done cocaine, but not IV ... they ... but the equivalent to a speed ball ... kind of an empowered feeling ... where you're kinda down and numb, but you got a lot of energy ... that was a good feeling, and then oblivion was a great feeling. and I kinda, I'd, you know, you have to say that the proof is in the puddin' I, I drank, I dropped downers. I did everything for oblivion, just to really knock myself out.

When asked how one gets addicted the men's views varied considerably. Some men believed they had a choice while others believed they did not. Some men talked about their belief in a genetic component and addiction as an inheritable disease. Similar to the extant literature, multiple reasons were offered by participants as they narrated their addiction processes: the influence of family, relationships, peer groups; in order to cope with stress; life's problems and to escape from reality; to overcome a lack of control; to feel normal; curiosity; and to overcome feelings of personal inadequacy, such as shyness or lack of confidence (Anderson 1991; Becker 1953, Denzin 1987a/b;Haas 2003; Kiecolt 1994; McIntosh and McKeganey 2002; Peele 1989; Taber 1993).

Summary

This chapter has highlighted participants' backgrounds, that is, what their experiences were like during their early years. Generally, most participants' early family experiences in some form or another had a significant impact on their future use/abuse of drugs and/or alcohol. The following chapter considers how participants became addicted and managed their lives during this time.

4

Addiction Experiences

I mean, literally, I've done pretty much anything and everything [in terms of drug use/abuse]. (D)

The previous chapter outlined participants' backgrounds along with a consideration of their lives before they started using/abusing drugs and/or alcohol. In this chapter, I explore participants' insights into their addiction experiences, as D notes above, which include the drugs that they used in their early addiction. Also summarized are the participants' personal views on how one gets addicted including their own relevant experiences within a drug and/or alcohol culture. I conclude with how they managed their addiction as they begin to think about changing their lives, thus exploring alternatives to their addicted selves.

Drugs Used in Early Addiction Experiences

Overall, out of the 25 men who were interviewed, there were only two participants who did not experiment with several other drugs. Blake explained that he had only used painkillers to which he became addicted, and JT mentioned that he "never got into any alcohol or marijuana or anything like that." One participant, Kid, explained that experimenting with different drugs is not synonymous with addiction. Although he experimented with several different substances, he was not addicted to all of them.

There were six participants who said there were few drugs they had not tried. Bierut et al. (2008) found in their study that in addition to cocaine use, the use of nicotine, alcohol, marijuana and other illicit drug use was the norm with the men in their study thus indicating that some men may engage in multiple substance use or polysubstance use, similar to some of the participants in this study.

Kid explained that he had "experimented with about everything out there." Leonard also talked about his experimentation with several drugs which included alcohol, heroin and various pills. Sterling also stated that:

> It might be easier just to tell you what I haven't done. I've never done needles, I don't like needles, but ice, whack, smack, crack, cocaine, whatever, I've done all that.

So, too, D commented that: "I'd be better off naming ones I haven't, honestly."

Duane also explained how he had used many different drugs as he commented:

> All pills, except for OxyContin, I tried 'em; they just didn't do anything for me. Some of 'em I didn't try again because they didn't do anything for me but those that worked I used.

Duane also used LSD as he explained: "When I lived in Texas, a lot, I would get a book ... 10 sheets and, uh, and I would sell it to the guys I was in the army with and, uh, mostly just eat it."

Aaron also used several substances explaining: "I did go on a rampage for about four years and I went through the drug system. I was able to consume, smoke, shoot up, anything I wanted, every type of pill form that you can think of." Aaron then became addicted to his drug of choice which was methamphetamine.

Other participants talked about how they had only experimented with a small amount of substances. Sherman had only used marijuana and crack cocaine. Timex had used alcohol regularly and had smoked marijuana prior to becoming addicted to his drug of choice which was methamphetamines. Trent had used acid, mushrooms, hallucinogens and had used cocaine on occasion. Harvey had used cocaine and alcohol consistently throughout his adolescence. Oliver had used marijuana and heroin but explained, "It just wasn't my thing." Recounting his experiences, Gorilla said: "It started out with alcohol, then to weed (which he used until his early thirties), and then I went to cocaine, tried Ecstasy one time."

Daved stated that he has used different types of pills and PCP. He also used marijuana: "I smoked it pretty regular into my early thirties." David stated that he had used "pills, speed, I tried, I was on them for a few years, drinking. I drink a gallon a day easy, and a case of beer, that was average." He continued:

> I would start from six in the morning or whatever since I woke up and a Coke, and I'd take a big old like McDonald's plastic cup ... and take it to work with a straw in it and sip on it.

Along with his drug of choice, alcohol, Martin had also used acid and mushrooms as he explained:

> Probably six months of just doing pot and then I started experimenting with other things, my best friend again, he grew up out in the country so the shrooms were growing all around, so he would just get 'em and we would try 'em. We would try acid just because we had access to it, why not?

The majority of participants stated that they had also experimented with numerous other substances. The men discussed the fact that they had begun experimenting with alcohol and marijuana which eventually progressed to different substances. Leonard mentioned that "all my barriers had gone down." And Duane noted "there isn't any drug that was ever put in front of me that I didn't try."

As participants began using different substances they were open to experimenting with new ones, thus mirroring McIntosh and McKeganey (2002) argument that one's escalating use can be driven by a continuing desire to experiment and find new "highs," as well as the need to satisfy ever rising tolerance thresholds. Participants found that they eventually preferred one drug over another. Although they may have continued to use other substances, their drug of choice was the one drug they favored to which they developed a strong addiction, as seen in the following section.

Men's Drug(s) of Choice

In this section I highlight participants' drugs of choice, the drugs and/or alcohol to which they finally became addicted. Table 4.1 shows the distribution of participants' substances of choice as they began to experience their addictive phase.

The primary substance of choice for 13 participants was alcohol. Marijuana was the drug of choice for five men, while nine had used meth. Other use was for cocaine (six) and two had also used heroin. Five men used acid/LSD as well as psilocybin mushrooms and OxyContin to a certain extent.

Table 4.1. Participants' Primary Drug(s) of Choice*

Drug(s)	Frequency percent	(n)
Alcohol	52.0	(13)
Marijuana	28.0	(5)
Meth	4.0	(9)
Cocaine	8.0	(6)
Heroin	8.0	(2)
Other	4.0	(5)

(LSD/psilocybin mushrooms/OxyContin)

* Numbers do not equal 100 percent as the participants often used the above drugs in combination with others.

For example, when asked about his primary drug of choice, Sherman said: "I loved smoking weed, I loved the high I get from weed but, uh, ever since I first tried crack, I've always loved that high from it." Although Sherman also enjoyed using marijuana, once he began to use crack it became his primary drug of choice.

Trent also described his experiences with several other substances that eventually led to meth as his drug of choice:

> All the acid and the little bit of cocaine, and all the mushrooms and a little bit of Ecstasy that I did was all before I hit meth, once I hit meth, I didn't want to do any other drug. I was a heavy pot head up until I started shooting meth, and then I found out that meth was so much better that I didn't want to waste my money or my time on pot anymore and I completely started doing meth. All other drugs including alcohol were off the board, you didn't want to do anything else.

Sterling also talked about experimenting with several different substances as he stated: "I would do anything. I didn't go out and buy stuff, but if it came my way or there was a sample I would do it." In time, he did find his drug of choice which was "pot."

Oreste talked about his primary substance, which was alcohol. He noted that alcohol was his drug of choice because:

> I was in college … tried marijuana and hash, um, I didn't like the sensation, I felt more out of control. The alcohol, with alcohol, I had a sensation at least cognitively; that I knew it was happening. I knew how far out of control I was.

D used morphine as well as methamphetamines, but when asked his drug of choice D responded: "I would say meth. Like I said, I did morphine for a while, and got addicted and it got bad, but I've never had to continue it, I mean, I used meth for years."

After the men discussed their drug and/or alcohol use in the early phase of their addiction, I asked participants how long they had been addicted to their drug(s) of choice. The following table highlights the number of years addicted.

Table 4.2. Length of Addiction in Years

Years addicted	Frequency percent	(n)
<10	20.0	(5)
10–15	36.0	(9)
16–20	16.0	(4)
21–25	16.0	(4)
26–30	4.0	(1)
>30	8.0	(2)
Total:	100.0	(25)

The number of years in which participants were addicted to their particular drug of choice varied among the men. For two men, their addiction lasted for over 30 years. Bishop had been addicted to heroin and cocaine since the age of 16. He had been an addict for 31 years before going into recovery. Oliver had been addicted to alcohol since the age of 21 and used regularly for 35 years as he said: "I started drinking, uh, every day when I was fresh out of the penitentiary … and I got out when I was 21." Oliver went into recovery at the age of 56.

When asked how long they had used Duane and David both said that they had used for approximately 20 years before going into recovery. Another participant, Daved, stated that he had used for "about 26 years." Bobo discussed the fact that he had used regularly for 21 years. He continued to use even when he was in prison:

> Normal everyday stuff you know, only breaks that I got was, when it really wasn't too much of a break, I mean going to prison, I mean I still smoked weed in prison.

When asked how long he had been addicted, Sterling responded by stating: "From when I was like 13, 14 all the way up until I was 30."

Travis also stated: "I started drinking when I was 12 ... I am 28 now – 16 years." Oreste said that for "15 years I used varying levels and amounts." Another participant, Buck, stated that he had used "from the age of 13 ... to about 23."

Aaron noted that he had tried to stop using drugs about three times but had been addicted to his particular drug of choice for around 13 years. Herb stated: "I stayed in that stuff for ten years, just living that lifestyle." Timex mentioned that he had been addicted to different substances for certain amounts of time: he had been addicted to methamphetamines for around ten years, while he used alcohol for two or three years.

Four participants were addicted for a period of three years or less: D, Blake and JT had been using actively for three years. One participant, Trent, noted that he had been addicted to methamphetamines for two and a half years. However, he differentiated between different times during his addiction. He mentioned that he had only used intravenously for about five months.

As highlighted in the foregoing discussion some of the men were addicted to particular substances for a considerable amount of time. The following section highlights participants' ages when they began using their substances of choice.

Ages at Which Men Became Addicted

Most participants became addicted during their teenage years. The following table highlights the ages when men self-reported that their addictive careers began in earnest. As Table 4.3 shows five men began their drug and/or alcohol use when they were less than ten years of age. Another 12 were between 10 and 15, a further five between 16 and 20 and three between the ages of 21 and 25.

Table 4.3. Ages at Which Men Became Addicted

Age of initial use	Frequency percent	(n)
<10	16.0	(5)
10–15	48.0	(12)
16–20	20.0	(5)
21–25	16.0	(3)
Total:	100.0	(25)

Stephens (1991) argues that addiction processes involve factors of a reference group nature and that (our) social behavior develops not only as we respond to the expectations of others and as we experience their norms, but also through the processes of social interaction with others. Therefore, it is not unusual that these participants in particular used in their early years with their peers and/or significant others.

The purpose of the following section is to explore how participants felt about themselves as they experienced what many termed, the "pleasure" side of addiction.

Pleasure within Addiction Experiences

> I loved it. [It] changed my life, right then. Before I drank I was just a scared nervous little kid, but it did something for me, and it changed my view of myself and everyone else, almost instantaneously. (Duane)

In this section, I explore how participants felt about themselves as they began addiction in earnest. Duane's explanation above mirrors many other participants' views in this study. Common descriptors emerged in men's lives during this time: For four of the men, using allowed them to forget negative feelings and problems they were having in their lives. For others, using made them feel like "the man;" using gave some a sense of empowerment and a sense of self confidence, the ability to become a risk taker, a lack of stress, a feeling of control, the opportunity to become "somebody else," and a normalization of their lives along with enjoyment in using.

Overall, participants described positive feelings and experiences that came with their drug and/or alcohol use. For example, Travis explained that he "had what everybody wanted. I was the man. Everybody who wanted some drugs knew where to find me – look for the big white truck." He further stated that

> Meth keeps me awake, makes me picky about the way I look, the way I act, the way I keep my truck, or my house, or my kids, or whatever, clean, you know, looking good.

Rock also described a feeling of empowerment: "It was fun and if you had a package, you was kinda like the king ... people looked up to me, having the power, having control."

For Bishop, drugs made him feel "euphoric, confident, relaxed, that is basically how they made me feel, very euphoric, very relaxed, real self-confident, it made me a great risk taker."

Buck also noted that using made him feel like everything was going well:

> It feels real good at first, you know, you get a lot done, you're not tired, you can work all the time, and [it] gives you a euphoric feeling well as the energy you get from it. When I didn't have no drugs, just drank, and I never came down, and I always, it just replaced it and just a different high ... it's a feeling of everything is alright, everything's good, nothing bad can happen, nothing matters, there's no stress.

Timex stated that using gave him a "hell of a rush." Trent also described his experiences positively and described the feeling as "like an orgasm times ten." He continued:

> All this energy that you never knew was even possible to have, you know ... and not being hungry, not having to feed yourself, just straight on through. The feeling that you get for that first five minutes, is such a, such a feeling you wanna repeat it. And if you had enough to do it again you'd do it right then again.

For three men, using allowed them to forget negative feelings and the problems they were having in their lives. Leonard initially described his drug use positively, "I love feeling an empowered feeling. You got a lot of energy ... that was a good feeling, and then oblivion was a great feeling." However, as he fell deeper into addiction, he aimed to quiet his feelings of inadequacy. He stated:

> I did everything for oblivion, just to really knock myself out. You know, the, the guilt and the ... the horrible feelings of not living a life or being addicted, got to a point where the ... you couldn't do enough drugs ... to quiet those feelings.

For Gorilla, using "took away that scared impending doom feeling" that he felt throughout his life. Aaron was able to become "somebody else. I liked it because it took me out of my frame of mind. I was somebody else, I could create any type of fantasy I wanted in my head and I became that person." Blake stated that "I felt that I needed it just to get through the day."

For Aaron, he liked his drug of choice because as he stated:

> It took me out of my frame of mind. I was somebody else, I could create any type of fantasy I wanted in my head and I became that person; if for example, I wanted to be Donald Trump, I'd do some LSD and I would feel, think, and act as Donald Trump. ... the money

to back me up. I liked it a lot, because I would do it on the weekends whenever I wasn't at work and I wanted to blow a whole weekend off and wanted to be by myself, always did drugs by myself, I don't like doing it with anybody else.

For one participant, Blake, there were no positive feelings associated with his use:

I didn't feel anything, I felt absolutely nothing. I just felt lucid, just, I was just in a daze, a constant daze. I would wake up from the bed and move directly to the sofa, and I didn't want to do anything. The only time I actually ever physically got up and did anything was when I needed to find more money.

The majority of participants interviewed described positive feelings associated with their drug use. For them, using drugs and/or alcohol made them feel empowered and euphoric. This stage in their use was a pleasurable one and they enjoyed their time with their drug of choice. The following section highlights the changes and adjustments participants made as they immersed themselves into their addiction.

Immersion into Addiction

I dropped every single friend in contact I had that was not using meth, because you had no desire to hang out with them because either they'd look down on you, which most of them did, or they just didn't want to do it and they didn't understand why you wanted to … so you wanted to hang around with people that either could get it more often or liked doing it like you and it was, it became a really, unfortunately, it became a really close circle of people that I was hanging out with, and they were all people that were on meth. (Trent)

Many of the participants made major changes and adjustments in their lives while using; in other words, they became immersed into a drug and/or alcohol culture as noted in Trent's comment above. Common descriptors among the men included the following: breaking ties with family members, with former friends who did not use drugs and becoming involved with other users; and becoming involved in illegal activities, such as stealing. In several participants' lives, prison, too, was an outcome of their using. Obviously, in many cases, participants' reference groups changed as they moved into the drug culture. Terry (2003) argues that the view of the reference group that we relate to the most acts as a lens through which we see the world, similar to how these participants were changing their worldview.

Men's Experiences within a Drug and/or Alcohol Culture

Although some men did not make any major adjustments in their everyday lives while using, for some participants, many things changed. Some immersed themselves in a drug and/or alcohol culture and did not associate with those who did not use. Others noticed that they were unable to do things they had always done. Some men, however, attempted to maintain their routine and everyday activities while continuing to use.

For example, Blake talked about being involved in "a lot of illegal activities." Blake explained that he was stealing in order to support his habit. Blake later found himself in jail after writing a "bad check" while trying to purchase a new vehicle.

A few men did not make any major adjustments in their lives and tried to continue their usual routines while using. Travis stated that: "I worked and worked, came home and worked." Harvey continued to study and attend school.

When asked about the impact of their drug use on their families and their relationships with others, some participants said that they continued to have relatively good relationships with their parents. For some, relationships were strained when those close to them first became aware of their substance use as shown by JT's comment that his mother "she pretty much wanted to write me off, you know." He stated that his mother had told him: "'Just don't come back around here until you're done away from that stuff 'cause I don't want it nowhere around my family,' um, and that kinda hurt too, but at the time I was too wrapped up." Through his addiction to methamphetamines, JT stayed close with his mother as she tried to help him.

D also talked about how his drug use strained the relationship he had with his mother and father:

> My mom wouldn't trust me in her house all by myself, alone. I've never stole anything from her, but she knew … she'd be like, "I don't want drugs in my house.'

D highlighted the fact that although his parents were understandably disappointed with his use of drugs, he respected his mom's wishes and stated that "I never lied to my family about it."

Bishop talked about a time in his life when he was incarcerated. He explained that he had married his wife in 1982, however, while in prison, she died of a heroin overdose: "That was a painful experience, more so for my children, my two daughters." For Bishop, it was harder to see his daughters suffer from the loss of their mother. Bishop was able to attend the wake yet he was so consumed with his drug use that "my whole thing of going to the wake was to have somebody else bring me drugs so I could get the drugs back in prison."

Sterling explained that his alcohol use did not have an impact on his relationship with his girlfriend at the time, in fact, she drank along with him:

> I had the same girlfriend all through high school and there after high school for awhile and she influenced me to drink a lot, she loved drinkin', her parents drank, and she was always sneaking into their liquor cabinet so, basically every night we would just go out and get drunk every single night and that's all we did.

Some of the men discussed how their friendship networks changed during the time of their substance use. For example, David talked about his initial belief that he had made friends with other methamphetamine users. However, he stated that often, users would steal from one another in order to get their drugs: "It was unbelievable and the people were so nice and you let them in your house and then they just steal from you right behind your back, it's unbelievable." David went on to say "I just, never met nobody that you could really trust." As a result, while using David never developed strong friendship networks with other users.

When asked if his friendship networks were changing at the time of his substance use, Travis responded: "Oh yeah, I'd say networks. I have only one really good friend." Although his friend was also a user, Travis noted that this friend eventually played a key role in his recovery.

For Martin, his friendship networks did not change significantly, yet he felt he became very isolated because of his drug use. Martin eventually developed a relationship with his pastor and members of the congregation because they "didn't judge [me], it, it was actually amazing to me. My youth pastor at the time, he really played a big role in helping me out."

Many of the men discussed the idea that while they were using, they were also immersed in a community of users. For example, Buck noted that all of his friends were fellow users. Martin also actively sought out friendships with other users:

> My friends actually changed, uh, when I got into high school ... I got
> more into using and they weren't so I had to find new friends that
> shared my interests and I did.

Sherman mentioned that whether he used alone or with others would
depend on the substance he was using. Sherman described himself as a
"closet" addict when it came to his use of crack cocaine. He did not
want to be seen as an addict as he mentioned that he saw how other
people would treat an actual addict so he never shared his "dope" with
anyone.

The majority of the men interviewed stated that they often
associated and used with others who were a part of the drug culture.
Procuring and using substances brought them into contact with other
users. Martin mentioned that individuals who do not use drugs and/or
alcohol may not understand an addict or the reasons behind their using,
thus prompting an addict to seek out relationships with fellow users,
similar reasons to other research in the area (Bahr et al.1995; Elliott et
al. 1985). McIntosh and McKeganey (2002) also found in their study
that the main reasons for participants' initial drug use were curiosity and
a desire to comply with the expectations of others, especially peers.

One issue that participants were obviously very aware of and which
was offered in our conversations was the fact that several of the men had
served time, either in prison or in jail. The following section highlights
this particular topic.

Prison and/or Jail Time for Participants

Thirteen participants had spent time in prison and five had served some
jail time. For example, Bishop had a litany of his experiences as he
stated that his reason for eventually being incarcerated was because:

> I hustled, I learned how to steal, pick pockets, steal out of stores,
> selling drugs, I sold drugs off and on throughout all my addiction and
> basically illegal sources and it didn't necessarily matter how it came
> about most of the time. I began to go to jail when I was, about when I
> went to Juvenile [Corrections] under the age of 18 a couple of times,
> but I began to do some real incarceration when I was about 18, 19
> years old.

Bishop continued as he clarified this time in his life:

> I was in for hard time a year or better, my first sentence was for three
> years and I was 19, 20 I think at the time and from then on it was just a

succession of getting out of jail, hustling on the streets traveling across the U.S. with a team hustling still and finding dope and using drugs, everything else came secondary it didn't mean that I didn't keep myself up, didn't dress, I always dress nice because part of the hustling that I did required that you be kinda of neatly dress, because it was mostly out of stores, I did that for many, many years and it got real good, it was exciting we took a lot of money out of different places, out of back rooms, safes, that kind of thing. So, that was my main hustle aside from that I sold drugs a lot, if I had the chemicals with me then I could fix myself and I would sell the rest of it and go back and get some more and fix myself and sell the rest of it and go back and get some more, over and over again.

As a result of such experiences, he:

Went to prison in Missouri five times, I had five separate incarcerations in the state of Missouri, those range from three years, my first incarceration was three years and the last time I got out, my last incarceration I was serving a total of nine years with various amounts of time in between, in other words I had a nine year sentence and I had two nine year sentences and two seven year sentences, two fives, a four and a two and they were all run concurrently.

He further expanded on this time for him:

Early on, prison for me, prison was part of my lifestyle; it was something along the way I expected to happen. I was prepared for it, when it did, not that I wanted to go but when I knew I was going it wasn't a big deal, prison for me was a place to go, clean up, come back out and do the same thing over again, or figure out a way to do the same thing over again.

Sherman had forged some checks and eventually served, "The first time – 5 ½ months, and then I was out about 3 months on house arrest. Then I got rolled back, I got sent back, back for 6 months on a violation. So, so, 11 ½ months total."

Bobo also served a total of 11 years for selling drugs, possession, deliveries and trafficking in drugs. Gorilla at the age of 30 also spent eight months incarcerated for using drugs.

David spent six years in prison at age 25, not for drinking but because he "Was an accessory with a friend who had committed a robbery with bodily injury." He further reiterated that he had not committed the crime himself but was picked up by the police because he was with his friend who had done the crime.

Buck also spent time in prison, 12 ½ months for a DWI (driving while intoxicated) and while there, took part in a rehabilitation program. Duane also completed four years in prison. JT spent time in a correctional facility for an alcohol-related offense when he was 21 years of age.

Aaron was another participant who was found guilty of assault with a deadly weapon and a count of assault on a police officer and at age 27 spent two years in a New York prison. So, too, Herb has been in and out of prison several times for events that were "alcohol related, like fights, or resisting arrest."

Oliver also spent time "in the penitentiary for violence – I cut somebody up one night." He was 18 years old at the time and spent three years and nine months inside.

Five participants talked about their time in jail. For example, Kid offered his experience:

> I was in jail and then of course jail led, jail led to … bonding out to DWI's which eventually led to prison, but I didn't actually go to, I went to prison until they got me into treatment, and when I say prison, it's a diagnostic center, it's where they … decide what camp you're going to or this or that … when you're going to treatment, it isn't like going to prison because prison, or DOC, Department of Corrections, don't have, they don't have jurisdiction on you; the judge still does. So I was under jurisdiction of the judge, who sentenced me to treatment, and both times, two times. One time in '96, I went to, done a 120-day treatment in the Department of Corrections, but it wasn't actually in the Department of Corrections, it was … it was a place to itself in prison.

Timex had spent time in jail both overnight and for several weeks:

> I've done overnights and two or three weeks, you know, for traffic tickets or violations or whatever, but I've been on paper three times felony, first two times was uh theft, theft, felony theft over $500.

And Sterling also spent time in jail a "few times" for DWIs as did Oreste and Daved.

This section has offered an overview of the prison and jail experiences with several participants. It is clear in this study that for a few of the men, one of the consequences of their using alcohol and/or drugs was their engagement in some type of crime (i.e., selling drugs, possession, deliveries and trafficking in drugs; forging checks, DWIs, being an accessory to a crime, alcohol related fights, assaults, theft and felony theft). Such experiences eventually helped in the men's processes of change as they considered recovery. Gorilla said it well when he stated: "Prison's a pretty good motivator" [for getting clean].

How do individuals manage their addictions and, in particular, how did these participants do so? The following section highlights this issue.

How Men Managed Their Addictions

How did the men manage their everyday activities while using? Answers varied among these participants. Several of the men interviewed were in fact able to maintain their everyday activities, like going to school or working while addicted. However, for others, their drug and/or alcohol use began to affect their everyday lives as highlighted in the following quotes.

Bobo is a participant who was able to balance his life with his substance use; he began using while he was still in high school, as he stated:

> I was just drinkin' and smokin' weed and I had to pick certain times when to do it, and when not to do it, you know … I went to school … pretty much every day, but I knew I had … I was in sports so I knew I had to maintain a certain grade average to keep playin' sports. I played football, basketball and ran track.

When asked if his coaches were aware of his substance use, Bobo responded: "Yeah, they knew … I had one tell me, 'just as long as it don't affect … my performance, or don't do it before the game,' which I still did, but I think … they didn't care because I was winnin' them games." Bobo went on to say "that's how I got to go to college, I had a full scholarship." Although Bobo used throughout his high school years he was able to maintain good marks and continued to be a strong athlete.

For Martin, attending high school while using was a struggle and his school work began to suffer. He stated that at least six days out of the week he was under the influence. He continued to explain how he was able to use while at school:

> We would do it outside or in the bathroom, it just depended. I went to summer school every year, um, and my senior year I actually had to go to summer school and night school because I wasn't gonna … graduate. I didn't get my diploma, I had to wait, um, the problem was, my junior and senior year after I quit using I was still so far behind cause the first two years I blew, I went just enough, that I wouldn't be held back, you know.

When Buck's parents passed away, he had to leave high school in order to care for his two younger sisters. He began working as a janitor during night shifts and used meth while doing so. Although Buck was using methamphetamines, he was able to continue working and providing for his sisters.

Trent had graduated high school and applied to college, but "you know, my parents ... they're great to me, and they wanted me to go to school or do something else." In his attempt to appease them he dropped out as soon as he found a way to not have to go to school by telling his parents that he was going to go into the navy.

JT, while using, was able to maintain a job with a tire company. He felt that he was making a decent amount of money; however, his habit was an expensive one as he relates:

> I was, uh, working for a tire company, doing semi tires ... we'd pull off the tires, off the semi-trailers and we'd fix them or replace them or whatever. I was making decent money, I was bringing home close to about $400 a week, um, but, when you spend $300 a week on drugs, you have a hundred dollars left for gas, cigarettes, and food.

Herb continued his usual job and did not consider the consequences:

> Oh I was a truck driver. I would still find, I would find a job long enough, you know, and then lie and manipulate my way into another one, to another one. Call a cousin or something and say, act like you're a company, and all this kind of stuff. So there was ways to get jobs. I never thought about the consequences.

David was also able to maintain employment: "I had one job in California I kept for 12 years."

Another participant, Aaron, also stated that he was able to work while addicted and felt that at the time, his addiction was under control. He talked about working small jobs:

> I started off painting while continuing my drug abuse. See, this is the thing about me, I felt that my drug abuse wasn't out of control because I can do meth, stay up for a week at a time, but yet I was still going to work. I wasn't missing any days and so I felt at that time that my drug abuse wasn't out of control.

Aaron noted that he would often drink at work but was able to hide it well. He stated that he was

Always drinking, swigging out of my water bottle. It's a colored water bottle so you couldn't see what was in it anyways, so some days I'd switch up from the vodka to Jagermeister or whiskey or whatever I felt like that day.

The reason he was able to hide it so well was that he was able to work by himself, not necessarily completely unsupervised but, as he stated, "with nobody hanging" over his shoulder, and no immediate co-workers who could smell it. Aaron, however, stated that he had once owned his own business; however, "drug abuse took that away from me too." Although Aaron may have been able to hide his substance use from others at work and continue to perform well, his use in the end affected his ability to work.

Travis also continued to work while addicted to methamphetamines. He explained that he would use consistently throughout his days at work: "I'd do probably up to a quarter gram in the morning, go on lunch, do a quarter to a half, come home that evening, do a quarter, whatever was left." Despite his efforts to hide his drug use, when asked if people had ever begun to suspect something at work, Travis responded:

Some people, but I usually chewed gum. I really could maintain myself at the beginning and more towards the middle but there – whenever I knew that me and my wife were having problems I'd do more just so I wouldn't have to think about me and her splitting up. And, yeah, people started noticing. You know, I'd have really big black rings around my eyes, not looking like I'd slept for a couple of weeks which I hadn't. I started having accidents at work, you know, I operated a fork lift at work, a skyjack, and other heavy equipment.

Travis noted that in the beginning, he was able to manage his addiction at work, yet, after a certain amount of time, it began to seriously impact his performance.

Although all the men suffered from their addiction, some seemed able to conceal their use from others in order to continue going to school or working. However, in listening to the men's stories, it is evident that for some, their addiction began to hinder their ability to continue engaging in such daily activities.

Following the men's stories about how they were managing their addictions and eventually finding that they were having difficulties doing so, the following section focuses on the men's changing selves – how they were finally thinking about changing their lives.

Thinking about Change

> I don't ever want to die in a penitentiary. I don't wanna grow old in prison, you know, so that was my pain, that was my bottom. When the pain gets great enough, then you become enough willing to do whatever it takes to stay clean. (Rock)

The men described different things that happened in their lives that made them begin thinking about recovery as Rock notes above. Participants eventually came to a phase in which they began to realize that the drugs and/or alcohol they were using either had run their course or were no longer working as they formerly had.

Participants now began to change how they felt about themselves. Slowly they had to deal with the effects of drugs and/or alcohol use and how it had affected them over the months or years they had been using. My purpose in this section, then, is to explore how participants eventually began to think about their recovery.

Elements of Beginning to Change

> I got to my lowest low; I've never been a violent man in my life, even going through high school and stuff. I blacked out and when I came to it I had three guys and a cop laying at my feet and that's, I was high, I was on meth at the time, I don't remember doing any of it, and I realized, I'm gonna kill myself or I'm gonna get killed if I continue to do this, and that's what really woke me up. (Aaron)

Similar to other participants' views in this study, Aaron's quote shows how he eventually "woke up" to the possible consequences of his life, thereby propelling him into his change process.

The following common descriptors emerged from the men as they began to talk about changing their lives from one of addiction to recovery: the fear of dying in prison, the fear of the consequences of their actions, being "sick and tired" of the lifestyle, health problems, and the realization of their crumbling relationships with family members. Some participants also described the important role of developing friendships and speaking with other recovering addicts as they contemplated recovery. Schwarzer (2001) argues that only individuals who become aware that their lifestyle puts them at risk may make a deliberate decision to refrain from risky behavior, such as drug use, similar to participants in this study.

As participants increasingly experience difficulties in their live, they begin to contemplate the need to change their use patterns and to initiate a process of self-change (Marlatt et al. 1988). Ebaugh (1988), Brown (1985), Biernacki (1986) and Ebaugh (1988) argue that the actual shift from the drug-addict role begins with a "turning point," a common theme narrated by the men in this study.

McIntosh and McKeganey (2002) identify some more common reasons given by addicts which promote their process of recovery; one reason is burnout, an exceptionally difficult and demanding task associated with many problems. Another reason is that they were "tired of the life" or words to that effect (Frykholm 1985; Simpson et al. 1986).

Further factors among the participants were deteriorating health or the fear of health problems (Simpson et al. 1986; Waldorf 1983), as well as the occurrence of more general negative events such as a period in prison or overdose or the death of drug-using friends/associates (Edwards et al. 1997), mirrored in participants' comments below.

For example, Nick grew tired of the consequences that came as a result of his drug use. He was also sick and tired of the lifestyle. Rock realized that his drug use would continue to land him in prison. He knew that the cycle of being released from prison and being sent right back would only repeat itself if he continued to use.

After suffering a stroke, Sterling saw the damage he was doing to his body: "This really did scare me because of what it did to my body you know, I couldn't even feel this side of my body for the first year." He noted that the key factor in his recovery was "the fear of dying." Sherman had gotten to a point in his life where he was so tired that he was okay with dying: "If I passed away within the treatment center, whatever, I just was tired, tired of doing what I was doing."

Herb explained that his fear of the tomorrow almost overcame him; he was afraid of going through life without alcohol as he commented:

> I had fear, fear of the unknown, you know, fear of, uh, having a Superbowl party without a keg of beer, that's ridiculous, there's no such thing, you know, you can't have a Superbowl party without beer. It was fear of this unknown, how are you gonna have fun on the weekend without some cold brew, you know ... how am I gonna enjoy life, I was afraid of tomorrow.

Yet, in talking about the key factor that led him to recovery, Herb further admitted that

It was the fear of continuing to live the way I've been living, you know, fear of death, fear of incarceration again, just, uh, fear of dying old in some cell, you know. I said there's only one option, get into recovery, open your mind, figure this out. You know, so I, I got humble, I got humble and I said look, I need help, I don't know what to do and I opened my mind and started taking these suggestions from these men and women, accepting these and trying them, like, call someone fine, I call somebody.

For some men, finally deciding that they wanted to change was the key to their recovery. Blake noted that something finally "clicked" when a former cellmate, who was also a drug user, warned him: "You don't wanna end up like me." Upon his second release from prison, Blake stated: "The only thing that was going through my mind was get a job, get your life back together." Another participant, Duane, chose recovery when he realized he just could not continue living the way he was any longer. For Duane, the key was to finally "surrender." As he stated, "Giving up the fight, I was beat, there was no going back in for another round, I was just beat."

Bishop felt that 12-step meetings and connections with other drug addicts helped him enter recovery as he stated:

I had no choice but to latch onto those individuals that were already in recovery who could tell me when I was facing something in my life. They could tell me, "Here listen, here's how I recently had the same situation in my life and this is what I did and this is how I got through it." It takes that parallel, that parallel, it says that one addict helping another is without parallel, you can't compare anything to that. And it's true.

Leonard also noted the importance of connecting with others in treatment. He went on to say: "I thought I was a bad person tryin' to get good and ... they told me I was a sick person tryin' to get well, and it really made a difference to me."

Other participants felt that family support was the key in their recovery. Some of the men realized that they were not only hurting themselves but also hurting those around them. Kid stated: "The key was realizing that it wasn't just me that I was hurting, that I was hurting others." Trent felt that family was the key to his recovery as well. He explained that he felt that it was finally time for him to do something for them: "Whenever I came home I was still living with my parents ... I guess I kinda had to do it for them ... they were the ones that were always there picking me back up." Bobo highlighted the fact that an addict must choose recovery for himself and not do it for others. However, he felt that "by me doin' it, that everybody else around me, they'd benefit from it."

Travis explained: "The key to my recovery would have to be the longer I stay clean the more chance I got to have my family back." Travis went into recovery in the hopes that his son and his wife would come back to him. Travis felt that he needed something to live for; he found that his reason to live was for his children.

JT believed that the key to his recovery was the support he received from others in his life. He explained:

> The key to my recovery was the timing, the people in my life … it was all just like it fell together like a puzzle, it was the last few pieces of the puzzle, everything happened right at the right time, the right moment to keep me away from it and stay away from it.

Bishop talked about going to prison. Often when he would be released he would simply go back to the gang lifestyle and eventually begin using again: "Well, normally when I got out, you know, the first I did was get with the gang to see what they are doing, it wouldn't be long before I was using, I didn't have an idea of getting out, getting a job, you know, it didn't cross my mind." However, on one occasion upon his release, he stated that "it was different this time because I was different in my heart. I thought differently this time." He went on to say:

> When I was in prison, of course I gave my life to Jesus Christ in July of '95, and I went to the treatment program, a long-term treatment program and that gave me some structure, it taught me a lot about responsibility and the biggest thing it gave me, a job that I began working while I was in prison that I kept when I got out. I had enough of this suffering and pain in jail and I began to practice some of the things the program was teaching me. You have to understand I was raised in a Christian home, as a child and I got away from that.

When asked why he had not contemplated going into recovery earlier, Bishop responded:

> I had kinda of accepted the fact that I would just die an addict. That is what I needed, that is what I was and I was going to be this person until I died.

The time came for Bobo when he realized that he was simply going through the jail system and wanted to change. Bobo was tired of going to prison and realized this would be the inevitable consequence should he continue to use. He commented:

> It all boils down to me … I wanted something different. It just opened my eyes, it's like, again it's like, no matter where you go, if you gonna participate in that, you still gonna get caught sooner or later. I've always heard that if you quit doin' this, you quit doin' this, it'll be better, but I didn't never try, and I was tired of prison … I was like "if I get out this time I'm, I'm not goin' back.'

For Bobo, it took him some time to realize that he wanted to stop going back to jail and that going into recovery could change that. "That's where my wife comes in, I mean, she showed me how to live and then she was always right there sayin' 'you don't have to keep doin' this.'" Bobo discussed the fact that the last time he was sent to prison:

> The first thing when I went back and, I just started readin' you know, I … I had a NA book … when I told myself I was like, man, if these people in these books can do it … it's just a light came on. Over time, I found myself getting more involved in the … in the treatment, you know, and I'm like, well, I'm doin' it now! I'm wakin' up today and doin' the things and readin' my books and doin' positive things.

Blake was also tired of the lifestyle and tired of being sent to prison. While in prison, Blake continued to have someone bring him drugs. However, while incarcerated the second time, the same person who had once brought him drugs was now incarcerated on unrelated charges. Blake stated:

> I always wanted to quit but I just couldn't, I absolutely could not quit, and, this was one of those opportunities where I could quit, basically, because I didn't have a choice at the time.

Now that he was in prison and had no contact on the outside to procure drugs while incarcerated, Blake saw this as an opportunity to stop using.

Rock was another participant who was also tired of going to jail. Rock noted that there were "several times I had been to prison, go to classes, go to meetings and get all the certificates, just to make it look good for the parole board." When asked why it had worked this time, Rock responded: "Because my pain had got great enough and I was sick and tired of the lifestyle I had been living and I really wanted to try something different." Rock talked about his sponsor that was also a recovering addict. Rock continued "I sat there looking at him and I had read in the book that 'if he can do it, I can do it.'"

Duane had first been arrested on drug related charges at the age of 18. Nevertheless, Duane continued to use and violated his probation:

> I only did four months and I got out and I went and saw the PO [probation officer] and he said, "Uh, you can't drink, you can't do any drugs, I want you to go to these meetings." The idea of doing that wasn't something I couldn't even entertain; I never even went back and saw that guy. Knowing that I was going to go back to prison when they caught me and that was just what happened.

Duane was sent back to prison and completed a portion of his sentence. Upon his release, Duane went right back into his drug use and tried to stay out of trouble with the law. While using methamphetamines on the streets Duane realized: "I gotta get out of here or I'm gonna die." Duane had once attempted to stay clean and had abstained from using drugs for two and a half years. At the time he had a sponsor who told him, "Duane … get a sobriety date and keep it." However, at the time Duane was not ready for recovery and began using again. It was not until he was arrested once again that he began to think about his sponsor, "and those words … it meant something to me."

Gorilla said it well when he stated: "Prison's a pretty good motivator." He explained that while he was in prison he had a counselor who was a recovering addict himself. His counselor had told him that he had been through a lot of painful events in his life himself, however, once "you get past all of the bullshit, the truth is, that you just like the feeling you get when you use." Gorilla continued:

> I was like, yeah, that's so true, you know when you get past all of the bullshit, that's the truth, so let's figure out how not to do that.

Buck also talked about prison influencing his decision to go into recovery. Buck made a conscious decision to quit after his third charge of driving under the influence. He explained that he had "never stole anything, never got in trouble for anything but the DWIs, and when I got the third DWI, and they started talking about sending me to prison I realized I better do something." Buck continued:

> I started going to church and meeting people at the church that were recovered addicts. Getting fellowship with these people was what sparked the, I needed to do something to change my life, it would keep me better.

When asked if one needs to be ready for recovery Buck responded: "You gotta hit rock bottom that's for sure, I mean, you ain't got nowhere to go but up."

For Harvey, recovery came with the realization that he only had two options: "It was either keep using or go to jail." Martin also realized that he had two options with the life he was leading as he stated:

> The key thing that made me decide to quit is my whole life I've always wanted to be a successful person, you know, not just financially, but just that whole American dream I guess, the wife, the great kids, and, and the dog, I have the dog, the wife, and the fence right now, but I don't have the finances or the kids. But I just looked at my life and I really started thinking at this pace, you know, where am I gonna be and the only answer I could come up with is, I'll either be dead or I'll be in jail.

What prompted Travis to start thinking about recovery was: "The feeling inside of me, watching my daughter and my wife load up their stuff in the truck and take off ... knowing that they would never, ever come back."

Trent talked about the negative impacts of his methamphetamine use: "I'd just been ... kicked out of the navy and you know here I am getting another drug charge so then again putting that on paper, you know, I wasn't helping myself that much." After being charged Trent realized the impact it was having on his ability to find employment. Trent stated that he made a decision and "completely swore off meth." He continued: "I don't even have a desire to do that anymore ... you see what the stuff's made out of, you hear what it does to your body."

Leonard made a conscious decision to just stay clean one day at a time. He continued his story:

> I kept waking up every morning, I literally, I would be crying ... I, I was sleeping between two buildings. I'm waking up every morning and just thinking, "Oh God I gotta stop." I started thinkin' about the fact that I was probably gonna end up dying ... and I, it was kind of scary to think that I wouldn't have lived a life ... and that I would've just died.

Sherman stated that he began to think about recovery seriously when he realized that he had to do it for himself:

> I got tired of doing the same thing over and over expecting something different, ah, I would go into treatment, when I first started going to treatment it was for my kid's mum. It was never for what I really need

to go there for. Or else it was just to get a sheet signed – to make it seem like I was going to do what I was supposed to be doing.

Sherman went on to say that he made the decision himself because "I didn't give a damn about a judge or anybody else truthfully. I didn't care about no one or anything."

D talked about a particular event in his life that made him consider going into recovery.

> It happened a day after a drug deal went bad. One of my friends got shot in the leg, I shot a kid in the shoulder, and, the next day I was mad when I found out that he hadn't died because he shot one of my friends. The more I thought about it, the more I was like "man, you're in a really dark place." My sister had been on me for like the last week or two before I left, because it was getting bad. I'd take a gun to my mom and tell her she needed to get rid of it. I really needed to change the way I was living my life. Took a duffle bag of clothes and went to my mom. Left everything behind.

Travis stated that his wife leaving him was the main reason he decided to go into recovery.

> I loved her too much ... I've been with this woman for nine years. We've been through high school together, junior high school, everything together. This is the woman I want to be with the rest of my life. And whenever I was using and drinking and everything, I didn't show her the love and affection that I needed to. I mean she tried so, so hard to get me to stop.

Bishop began to think about recovery while he was incarcerated, when he learned that his wife had overdosed on heroin: "I think that had a lot to do with me wanting to change, because I began to think hard about my children and them not having a father or mother through all those years." Bishop continued saying that the world he lived in was nothing but "smoke and mirrors ... I was very well known, and respected and recognized but none of that really meant anything. When I got honest with myself I realized that that didn't mean anything – that I didn't have to be that person anymore." Bishop also talked about a friend who played a role in his recovery:

> He'd been a heroin addict all his adult life and he turned his life around, he went to Atlanta, got his ministry degree, came back to St. Louis and has a very large church going right now, he became a bishop and they were bringing services into the institution. I was going to

church then and I went to his service and after he got to preaching he called me up and something just struck me – if he could do it, I can do it too and he told me I could.

The men discussed different factors in their lives that were the key to their recovery. For several men it was the fear of continuing to live a destructive lifestyle and the fear of its consequences. Some were afraid of dying alone in a prison cell. For others, the key was making strong connections with other former addicts and realizing that they were also capable of change. Several men also felt that their families played a key role in leading them into recovery. The men all talked about a key factor that led them into recovery. However, we see that these factors can vary and that there is no single factor that leads addicts to choose recovery.

How did participants tell others that they were struggling to enter their recovery and how were they treated within their community of users? The following section highlights the men's answers.

Often when addicts use they are part of an alcohol and/or drug culture. They may use with others, sell drugs or may even be involved in the production of illicit substances. And so, when they make the choice to stop using, this decision may not only affect them but also affect others. Some men talked about the negative reactions of others when they learned of their decision to stop using. Others described the positive reactions of their friends and family.

For example, D explained that he had to defend himself physically from others who were angry he had decided to stop using:

> I avoided my friends. I've actually gotten into a couple fights, defending myself from friends. People that were pissed off that I don't do this anymore, or people that, you know, "Oh, now you look down on me." No, I don't look down on you; I just can't do that anymore.

When D was addicted to methamphetamines, he became involved with others in the production and sale of meth, and as he was preparing to enter his recovery:

> One of the kids that I cooked with found out that I was leaving when I left, and, he was the only person that I told. Everyone knew we ran around together ... so he got stuff from it too, on my name because I just left. I've got people I owe money to, that it's not good when I see him. So, I've gotten into a couple fights with him.

There were two participants who noted that the reactions of others were not so supportive in the beginning. However, they became more positive when they saw that they were serious about quitting. When David first told his mother that he had stopped using she did not believe him. His wife had to convince his mother that he was no longer using.

Buck explained that his family was not supportive in his initial decision. In his past attempts to get clean, Buck had tried to force others into sobriety as well:

> I told them that I was, and ... they weren't real comfortable with it. The first time I went into recovery, I was gonna take everybody with me and, after that, you know, they hated it! When I first told them, they didn't want nothing, you know, "If I'm going into recovery, you're gonna quit doing drugs and alcohol too." That took me years to learn that wasn't gonna work.

Travis also experienced negative reactions from others. Friends and family had heard that he had joined a recovery program. When he told them he was no longer using "they didn't believe me at all, yeah, they was all laying bets, [saying] 'I'll give it a day, I'll give it a week.'"

Three participants explained that they had not told their families of their decision to stop using and rather they showed them. Sterling did not tell people he had decided to stop using, but turned down their offers to go out and drink:

> People would ask, "Hey let's go and get drunk or whatever" and I would just say "No man, I'm too scared to do that." They understand why after what happened yeah, yeah they don't think any less of me.

(Sterling had suffered a stroke and people understood his decision to stop using.)

JT did not tell others that he had stopped using, but they realized it when they saw the differences in his behavior and appearance. JT described his experience as a positive one:

> They could pretty much, see, uh, the look on my face, noticing that I gained some weight, um, I could actually finish sentences. Yeah, basically, I just, I did my own thing, I got away from it ... when it was time for me to show 'em, all I had to do was show up and they knew. I actually was smiling, you know, and something changed in my life.

Harvey also explained that his family saw a positive change in his behavior. "My family knew because, because I changed, I started acting normal."

The men described different experiences when they decided to tell others that they had stopped using. For some, their decision to stop using also affected others, who in turn reacted negatively. Some men literally had to defend their sobriety. Yet some participants described the positive reactions of their friends and family and noted that they were supportive of their decision to quit. One of the most important predictors of quitting drug use/abuse is having something to lose (e.g., friends, health, job) if substance use continues (Costello 1975; Havassy et al. 1993; Vaillant 1983/1995), obvious in some of the participant's experiences as revealed in this study.

This section has highlighted how participants finally had begun to consider stopping their use of drugs and/or alcohol and some of the varying feelings they were having about themselves that compelled them to begin to do so. Even though there were common characteristics among most of these men, perhaps Rock stated it most clearly when he stated that he was willing to try something new in his life:

> I just wanted to do something different with my life. I was tired of going to jail, I was tired of using drugs, I was tired of the whole lifestyle and I wanted to do something different. While in prison I took the [recovery] program to heart and I went to meetings on a regular basis, I got a NA book, I identified with the book. I was willing to try something new.

Summary

In this chapter, I have explored participants' insights into their addiction experiences which included the drugs and/or alcohol that they used in their early addiction. Also summarized were participants' personal views on how one gets addicted including their own relevant experiences within a drug and/or alcohol culture. I concluded with how they managed their addiction as they began to think about changing their lives, thus exploring alternatives to their addicted selves. The following chapter provides an overview of findings as they relate to participants' recovery experiences.

5
Recovery Experiences

I think another thing, that keeps me in recovery, is all the death that
I've seen from it ... my mother and all ... my wife's mother, and I had
like three friends die on me, doing drugs, and my parents both died
from alcohol. I don't want to see any of my family members die like
that, the kids and stuff, you know. (Buck)

In the preceding chapter, I explored participants' insights into their
addiction experiences. Highlighting Buck's quote above, this chapter
presents findings gathered from participants as they narrated their
recovery experiences.

As DiClemente, Schlundt and Gemmell (2004) suggest, the focus of
addiction researchers and practitioners has shifted from whether
addicted individuals change to how they change. Understanding the
process of change helps us ascertain key influences that promote change
and increase recruitment, retention, and the successful cessation among
substance abusers. Motivation plays an important role in recognizing the
need for change, seeking treatment, and achieving successful, sustained
change for all substance abusers. DiClemente et al. (2004, p. 103) argue
that

Motivation refers to the personal considerations, commitments,
reasons, and intentions that move individuals to perform certain
behaviors. Addicted individuals appear to be pushed or coerced at
times by these motivational forces, but at other times pulled or led by
them. Nonetheless, intentional human behaviors are considered to be
motivated, whether one's theoretical perspective views behavior as
shaped by contingencies, driven by unconscious motives, or directed
by self-regulation.

Overall, motivation is viewed as an important component
throughout the entire process of change (DiClemente at al. 2004).
According to Miller and Sanchez (1994), an important shift in thinking
and in examining motivation suggests that "motivation is not simply a

characteristic of the individual, but rather the product of interpersonal exchanges" (p. 55). A person's level of motivation is determined not by his individual strength but by external situations and by the people with whom he interacts. Further, motivation is better understood as a characteristic of environments and relationships than as a trait of individuals (Miller and Sanchez, 1994). Similarly, Simoneau and Bergeron (2003) argue that the settings and the people one interacts with both affect motivation. Deci and Ryan (1985) also contend that internal motivations to abstain from future drug use and drug-addictive behavior are major components in changing individual behavior. Therefore, in this study motivation is defined as the intentions, desires, goals, and needs that determine participants' behavior.

As detailed below, for participants, motivations to consider recovery came from different situations they experienced and various important individuals in their lives. First, in the following discussion I highlight participants' beginning processes of change as they consider recovery through shifting self-images.

Considering Recovery

> [I had this] fear of continuing to live the way I've been living, you know, fear of death, fear of incarceration again, just, uh, fear of dying old in some cell, you know. I said there's only one option, get into recovery, open your mind, figure this out. (Herb)

As Herb suggests, other participants' responses mirrored his comment as they considered their recovery. Participants related that they were beginning not only to see a different world for themselves but also to feel "different" from previous selves. According to McIntosh and McKeganey (2002) processes of identity are evident in individuals' efforts to distance themselves from illegal drug use; distinguish between the person they believed themselves to be at heart and the person they felt they had become because of their drug use and provide convincing explanations for their recovery. The following discussion illustrates how the men made initial decisions to end addiction, a process by which they began to redefine their drug and/or alcohol-using experiences.

Shifting Self-Images

> Recovery is the recognition of exactly how bad your addiction is, the pain it is bringing to others and recognizing what you have to do in order to eliminate the act of addiction in your life. (Oreste)

In this phase of the recovery process, as discussed below, the men highlighted how feelings about themselves changed as they resolved to leave addicted selves behind. Participants used descriptors such as the following: unmanageable lives (being out of control), wanting something different in their lives, deserving a better life, time to quit, and ultimately realizing the pain they were causing others as Oreste clarifies in the above quote. Biernacki (1986) argues that abstinence occurs for addicts as they have burned out, are tired of the life, and fear going to jail. Such individuals are experiencing role strain – a felt inability to continue to enact the requirements of the addict role and lifestyle. Biernacki (1986, p. 53) further argues that

> Some addicts … resolve to change their lives and stop using opiates when the option of continuing to use drugs entails consequences that are simply far too undesirable in terms of their view they have of themselves and their future lives. At this point, they rationally weigh each possibility and decide that they have much more to gain by breaking the addiction than by continuing it.

For example, Kid noted that this time, he was "looking at what it has done to my, my family, and what it has taken away from me." He highlighted particular events in his life that influenced his decision:

> I was prayin' to God, that he would intervene and help me because I was comin' home in a black out stage every night. I knew I, that my life had become, when I say my life had become unmanageable, pretty much, I mean, I was going, I was gettin' ready to go through another divorce and I was drinkin' every night, comin' home in a black-out state, not knowin' how I got home, not knowin' where I went, what I done.

Kid realized that his life and his addiction had become unmanageable. Coming home every night and losing consciousness because of his drinking was evidence that he was no longer in control.

Trent also made his decision to stop using substances when he decided that he deserved a better life. He commented:

> You have to realize that there is something better out there, and you
> have to start stepping up those stairs to get to that something better,
> you know, and drugs have always been an escape to not have to take
> those steps, you know. That's what the drugs did, they made you
> content where you are, you didn't, you didn't want to take a step up,
> you know, there was no reason to, you're happy where you were.

Trent continued saying that he concentrated on getting used to the
changes and going to school again which helped him in his recovery.
Both Kid and Trent describe particular events in their lives that played a
role in their decision to enter recovery. For these men, these events
showed them that they were losing control of their lives and their
addiction. Although these events marked a low point in their lives, they
were ultimately helpful in leading them into recovery.

The participants also talked about different events or individuals
who helped them make the final choice to stop using drugs and/or
alcohol. Some participants were finally able to look around and realize
the effects that their substance use had on others around them. They
were able to see what their substance use had taken away from them.
Some of the men realized that they deserved better lives than they were
living. A few of the participants also noted that religion helped them
choose recovery.

When asked how he made his final decision to quit, Bishop stated
that one must be ready to change and must want something different.
Bishop went on to stress the fact that one cannot be forced to stop using:

> They [other people] can't tell you to do it ... It comes from inside you.
> You've got to reach a point in your life where you say, you know, I
> want something different and you have to really mean it, I'd guess
> you'd call it surrendering.

Rock also talked about realizing that he wanted something different
out of life. Rock explained that a treatment center helped him make his
decision:

> Going to that long term treatment center it was totally different from
> being in any other institution I had ever been in, this program gave you
> a chance to really look at yourself and ask yourself, you know, what
> do you want to do with your life, you know, and so that's where my
> start took place then, you know, because I looked over my life history.

Rock asked himself: "What keeps sending me to jails and institutions?"
He realized that it was from:

Using drugs, because I use drugs, I commit crimes, I go to jail, so for 25 years that's all I ever knew, so this time around, I was in a, I was sittin' there and I was sick and tired of livin' like I was livin' and I wanted to try anything other than what I was always been doin' ... because my way of doin' stuff don't work.

While in prison, Gorilla decided that he wanted more out of life and knew he deserved better. After being released from prison, Gorilla stayed in a clean and sober house and attended meetings. This allowed him to begin the road to recovery. Sherman also grew tired of his lifestyle and decided he wanted to make some changes, finally aware of the fact that there could be something better for him in life as he said:

I just said ... I'm tired of how life is, and I know that, that my higher power has something better for me and I just got tired of doing the same thing over and over.

When discussing the time when he made his final decision to quit, Oreste admitted "it was desperately hard to quit until I reached the point ... the hardest part was wanting to quit." He continued:

It's one thing to scream I want to quit, I hate this because you're feeling the pain of everything you're feeling, but when you really want to change in your heart of hearts. There's a difference between the two.

What eventually helped Oreste was the love of his family and the recognition of what addiction was doing to his life.

David made his final decision when he finally realized what he was losing: "I knew it was going to kill me. I knew I was losing everything and then if I kept on it I would either die from it or lose my job and be living in the streets." David had not realized this earlier because he had never really sobered up enough to think about it. David's addiction also caused his wife to leave him. She had always said that if he stopped using she would come back to him. And so, he "just woke up one day and never went back to it."

Herb stopped using after he got into an accident with his daughter: "I could of killed my daughter that night, that accident, I could have easily killed her, and that seeped in and it's just, I said I gotta do this for my baby." His daughter's mother was also unable to care for their daughter; their daughter was subsequently taken away. Herb decided that he needed to stop using in order to be a good father for his daughter.

Travis also talked about an incident that made him realize he needed to be there for his daughter. He had taken a large amount of pills and had to be taken to hospital:

> They were pumping my stomach; they thought I was going to OD. And I stayed a week in the hospital and then during that week my ex-wife came up here and seen me with my daughter and she basically just put my daughter right there saying, "Do you want to grow up, do you want your daughter to grow up seeing you like this?" You know, and all I could do was look at her and my daughter and just cry, just cry. I've not used since.

For a few men, religion played the key role in their decision to stop using substances. Buck noted that although he and family members abused alcohol, "finding Jesus, finding the Lord" really helped him go into recovery and gave him the ability to abstain from using substances. Martin also stated that he had been raised in a Christian home and he chose recovery when: "I decided that the best way to live my life would be to live it for God and have a relationship with him, so I chose that and from that moment on I never wanted it again."

JT had made several attempts at going into recovery before being successful:

> My first initial, uh, effort, trying to quit wasn't very successful. The third, and fourth, and fifth time weren't very successful. And, you know, I've tried just moving away from it, and went back to it.

JT made his final decision to stop using after a close friend made a particular comment toward him:

> My friend, I've known for years probably, close to 15 years now, um, she looked at me, she goes "You know, you're a child, you need to grow up." And for some reason, right after that, just something clicked, I'm like, "I do need to grow up, this is childish, what am I doing?" I wanna become more of a grown up ... I told her I said "I don't know if I need help or not, but I want to stop this crap." I realized how stupid I was acting, and watching everybody else around me that was involved in that kind of a situation, they were all living really bad lives, going to jail, going to prison.

Duane chose recovery when he found that he could no longer go through life the way he was: "I was beat, I was beat, there wasn't any more ideas about how I could control it." Duane chose recovery after several failed attempts at taking his own life.

David had been suffering from addiction for several years but noted that he felt his recovery period was short. He made his final decision to stop using and did not relapse. He does feel that his recovery is an ongoing process and that he will continue to be in recovery for the rest of his life. He felt that recovery is definitely "an everyday, twenty-four-hour thing."

The majority of participants felt that recovery is an ongoing process and that they would continue to be in recovery for the rest of their lives. For some, there were certain experiences in their lives that finally led them into abstinence. As various scholars have argued (Denzin 1987a, b; Brudenell 1997; Haas 2003; Van den Bergh 1991) addiction and recovery are processes that occur over time and involve psychological, physical, cognitive, emotional, and spiritual changes. Such processes involve both internal and external changes; they are continuous processes that do not take place in a vacuum (Abbott 1995; Denzin 1987b; Underhill 1991) and involve conscious changes in individuals' life directions (Smith 1991). Neale, Nettleton and Pickering (2011) contend that individuals process their recovery journeys within the context of the complex social, material, emotional and discursive resources available to them.

So how did these participants see themselves as they processed the beginning of their recovery? Did their identities change, did their sense of self change, and, if so, how? The following section answers this question as the men highlight their changes.

Choosing New Identities and New Selves

> Drugs are just drugs. Drugs are going to always be drugs. What changes are the people who use drugs, so I know today that I have a choice in that matter. (Bishop)

The majority of participants felt that they had gained a new identity and admitted that they had to change who they once had been as Bishop clarifies above. McIntosh and McKeganey (2002) suggest that identities that have been seriously damaged by addiction and the addictive lifestyle can stimulate addicts "to restore their identities and establish a different kind of future for themselves" (p. 152), similar to the participants in this study. Singer (2004, p. 438) also points out that

> To understand the identity formation process is to understand how individuals craft narratives from experiences, tell these stories

internally and to others, and ultimately apply these stories to knowledge of self, other and the world in general.

For several men, it was clear to them that they had gained a new identity and a new self since they had stopped using. For example, JT explained that he "was trying to hide behind the meth." While using, JT was afraid to leave his house for fear that others would notice his behavior and identify him as an addict:

> When I using I was afraid to come outside because the neighbors might see me, you know, they could, you could tell sometimes, that just the way you're acting, if you're fidgeting with everything and you can't just sit still long enough.

He feels that he has become a different person and is no longer afraid of how others will perceive him.

Bobo described himself as "a whole different person" in recovery. Bobo felt that he was very selfish while using. He described little things like holding a door open for someone, or letting someone go ahead of him in a line. These were things he never did while using. He explains: "I mean I care for people now, I really think about how they ... about their feelings."

Rock felt that he had gained a new identity. Even as a child he explained that he did not have a lot of confidence and had very low self-esteem:

> My new identity, new sense of self for me is more positive now, more active and more of a people person in a positive way. You know, my self-esteem now is much greater than it's ever been, you know. I feel good about me. I didn't before, 'cause growing up I always ... I was too dark, my hair was too short or I didn't have the clothes, the right clothes, you know.

When asked if he felt he had gained a new identity, Aaron responded:

> You do, you always do, anybody you should ever talk to should say yes on that because your old self, your drug self or your alcohol self is what you're leaving behind at that door, you have to find yourself and who you are.

Aaron explained it well when he stated you have to "come to terms with it and find out who you really are beyond the drugs and alcohol."

When Bishop was asked if he had gained a new identity, he responded:

> Oh yeah, I met several other people that I've known for years that have changed and it kind of gave me some hope I guess. I guess that is what it was – there was some realization that there was some hope that I didn't have to be this person anymore.

David stated that his life had changed as well. For David, being free from addiction made him feel good about himself and what he was now doing. Kid explained that "You have to try to find you. So you have to try to find that person that should've been."

Travis felt that he had gained a new identity. He explained that:

> I can actually hold my head up, I'm proud of who I am, I am not; I am not a drug addict or alcoholic. I am doing something with my life.

Buck also felt that he has gained a new identity. He expanded: "I can say good things about myself now, when before I couldn't, and that's one of the things we do every Tuesday when we meet, we, everybody says their name and says something good about themselves. Now I can think of a good thing about myself."

Herb also believed that he gained a new identity for himself:

> Myself and self-worth was worthless, now myself is worth something to family, society, you know. My identity is not that guy. I am no longer that damn Herb.

Three participants felt that they did not take on a completely new identity when they entered recovery. They explained that they still felt like the same person, however, they felt that they were somehow "restored," or a "better" version of the person they had always been. For example, when asked if he had gained a new identity upon entering recovery, Oreste felt that he had not gained a "new" self but rather, a "restored" self. He explains:

> I don't think you get a new self, I think you get a restored self, in the way, in the way that somebody, um, finds a '57 Chevy that was in a barn somewhere and they restore it. And it may never be what it would have been if it had never been restored like off the line, but it's a darnn precious beauty when it's fully restored.

Martin felt that an individual's personality stays the same, basically who you are stays the same. But he clarified that one's thoughts have to change. He explained that one will change how they self-identify:

> You probably identify yourself in a different way, like I'm not this person that uses this anymore, or is addicted to this anymore, I'm now this person.

Nick felt that he did not gain a new identity since leaving the use of drugs. He explained that he had always felt confident and had high self-esteem: "I was the type of person that enjoyed life, loved life, ah, ah, love, see, I like to be around a lot of people." He explained that he just knew that some things had to change in his life and it was time for him for recovery.

Some men described their old self as inconsiderate and selfish. For example, Duane stated that drug addicts are takers, selfish and self-centered. When asked if he felt that the self changes, he responded: "Priorities change ... character changes, absolutely character changes." He expanded:

> When it comes down to character, before I had all of these ideas of the person that I wanted to be and my grandfather was that example of, of how man is supposed to be and they were good decent qualities and I wanted to be that and every time I wasn't able to live up to that I felt a little bit worse about myself and today I'm able to – and I can't, I'm not near the man my grandfather is, but I'm a whole lot better than I used to be and yet I'm still the same guy and all of that stuff that I went through and did was necessary for me to become the man I am today and I've learned to accept all of who I am, the good and the bad, whereas before I couldn't accept it.

Several participants felt that they now saw themselves differently than they once had and felt that they had gained a new sense of self in recovery. Herb felt that he did see himself differently in recovery. However, in the beginning he noted that he was afraid of his new self. Herb explained:

> I was afraid of him because I was like "man this is not my image," but then, as I changed my people, places, and things and started getting surrounded by different people and I found out it's okay to just be a nice guy, there's rewards to this here, you know.

When asked if he now saw himself differently, Bishop responded: "Absolutely." He talked about a friend who was entrenched in the drug lifestyle for years. He witnessed him change his life which, in turn, gave him hope. He realized that there was also hope for him and that he no longer had to be the person he was.

Oliver also stated that he now saw himself differently. He explained:

> I'm worth something today, I'm worth something today. I despised myself when I was addicted, I, I wasn't worthy of the time of day, I wasn't worthy of the food I was eating, I was the waste of humanity, and I hated myself. Self-esteem is out the window when you're actively addicted, there's, there is no such thing, not at least in my belief.

Now in recovery, he saw himself in a more positive way: "I don't have that self-hatred, you know, because of what I am, I am an alcoholic, but I'm no longer addicted, you know what I'm saying." Sterling also began to see himself more positively and realized that he had to learn how "to get high on life."

Trent felt that he did see himself differently. He noted that he wanted to change who he was, and in order to enter recovery, he felt that change was inevitable:

> A person has to want to change; you can't force them to or anything like that, they have to want to break the habit. You want to change yourself for the better because there's always something better than drugs.

Kid also saw himself differently and felt that he is now a better person than when he was using as well as a better father, a better brother, a better member of society, and better to himself.

Another participant, Travis, also felt that he did see himself differently. He noted that one can be successful if they are committed to changing their lives. He explained that his new self is:

> Happy, encourageable, ah, rambunctious. I think that's the word I'm looking for, ah, I always laugh, I have a good time all the time. You know, I can look my kids in the eyes, you know, that's the biggest part for me.

Blake also stated that he was "a whole different person than I was before." He continued:

> On the outside I probably look the same as I did. But inside, I mean, sometimes I just get sick of thinking about some of the things I did,

just to get the drugs, just some of the, you know, the pain that I put other people through.

Buck was another participant who began to see himself differently in recovery. He described his old self and his new self:

My old self was very selfish, very selfish, uncaring, and just self-centered, I just wanted what would make me feel good; I didn't care what other people wanted, or what other people needed, as long as I got what I needed, and now I care what other people have, what they need, and a better appreciation for life, and what to do with it, instead of just wasting it. I mean, I was to the point where, I didn't care if I died or lived, you know. And that's what it took for me to come into where I wanted to, I wanted to do it, instead of somebody else saying I had to do it.

D explained that his outlook on life changed once he had entered recovery. He also learned how to deal with different issues more constructively. D identified with a new sense of self. He explained:

Everything is so muted with the drugs that you do, that I don't think you ever have a clear idea of who you are without the drugs. Sometimes they talk about recovery, that you never really understand it until you're in recovery, because you never have to deal with this "self" thing. Okay, your "self" never has to deal with anything, you know.

D explained it well saying: "Other people saw me as a drug addict, people saw me as a convict ... so what did I do? I did drugs, I went in jail, and I fought a lot, you know, and now people look at me differently, and that influences how you look at yourself."

Duane did not feel that he had gained a new sense of self as yet:

It takes a long time; I'm not quite there yet. I'm still the same guy that did all those things and I can't, um ... I can't undo any of that, and I have to take responsibility for that, especially if I want to get better, take responsibility for that.

Harvey also did not feel that he had gained a new sense of self. He noted that he still felt like the same person, however, he felt that he had changed in terms of his actions. And also stated that he had more control over the choices he makes in life.

Maruna (2001) argues that for offenders to maintain abstinence from drug use and criminal activity, they need to make sense of their lives: they need to understand why they are now "not like that anymore" (p. 7). The majority of participants felt that they indeed saw themselves differently now that they had entered recovery. They described their old selves as selfish and self-serving. Now in recovery, they identified with a new sense of self and began to see themselves more positively. Granfield and Cloud (1999) contend that addiction and recovery processes consist of transformations that can be understood as ongoing processes of interaction through which people adopt new meanings and new self-images, similar to the experiences of these participants. So, too, do Brown (1985), Biernacki (1986) and Ebaugh (1988) argue that the actual shift from the drug-addict role begins with a "turning point." They further state that these "points" are characterized by an event that serves as the end to one role and the beginning of a new one (Anderson and Bondi 1998). Such "turning points" are an essential step on the road to recovery from addiction (Ebaugh 1988).

Biernacki (1986) and Anderson (1991) argue that as an individual enters recovery, not only is there a self-change, but also an identity transformation, or an "alternation" (Travisano 1970, p. 606), oftentimes described as "a radical reorganization of identity, meaning, and life" (Travisano 1970, p. 535). It is the process of changing one's sense of root reality (Heirich 1977), mirrored in the participants' lives in this study.

Obviously, new activities are vital to the establishment of new identities. Recovery can be understood as an ongoing process of interaction through which people adopt new meanings and new self-images (Granfield and Cloud 1999). McIntosh and McKeganey (2002) also argue that strategies need to be put in place in former addicts' lives in order to "manage one's desire" (p. 125) for the former drug(s) of choice. Strategies reflect the conscious activities participants were engaged in as they broke away from addiction and were necessary components in their recovery (Kiecolt 1994). Therefore, participants had to implement strategies in order to manage both their use of substances and everyday activities.

Overall, one's new life is being built with new adjustments, incorporating new activities, new commitments and new relationships. Such major adjustments for the men in this study are highlighted below.

Major Adjustments in Men's Lives

> I had to stop going to parties ... I figured instead of being tempted I might as well do something productive. I distanced myself from my old friends ... but slowly I made new friends. (Martin)

When asked if they had made any major adjustments in their lives once they had stopped using, the men talked about having to cut ties with friends who were still active users, similar to Martin's response. Some also talked about how they stopped frequenting certain places like bars or former friends' houses. Some of the men also moved away from where they had lived while using.

For example, Travis had to leave his current girlfriend because she wanted to continue using. Kid also stated that he had to change "my bad friends. Not that they're all that bad, but they're bad for me." Kid too had to stop associating with friends who continued to use in order to stay sober and that he had to change some of the places he used to go to, such as his local pool hall. Sherman also commented that he

> Stopped doing the same things, such as hanging around negative people, I stopped going around the same places. Like going to clubs and stuff like that ... if I go to a club now, it's like with my family to see, uh, a band or something like that.

In order to stay in recovery, Harvey also stopped seeing all those he associated with while using. Bobo moved away from the area where he had lived while using. He made significant changes in his life, admitting that he had never had to pay bills and had never had a bank account. Now, with the help of his wife, he is learning how to handle his new responsibilities. D also explained that he moved away from everything he knew:

> I left my house, my truck, left everything I owned behind. It just wasn't my friends, I left everything, 'cause I couldn't afford it, I was buying a house, I was buying a truck, I couldn't afford what I was doing, without the drug money.

When Leonard made his decision to stop using he noted that "everything changed." Leonard explained that it was not necessarily a change in his surroundings but within himself as he tried to adjust with himself and with society. He expanded on his thoughts:

Well I went from … I dunno know, I went from someone who hated himself and society, to someone who tried to adjust with himself and society. In my addiction … I am a pessimist, I'm a depressive, I'm a … a cynic … a critic … and in recovery I'm an optimist … I look for, the glass is half full of course, and I try to see the good in everybody that I come in contact with...and hope for them in their personal growth … so that they meet whatever it is they need. The … well, you know, I thought I was a bad person tryin' to get good and … they told me I was a sick person tryin' to get well, and it really made a difference to me … it was a concept that I could grasp.

JT also saw a change in himself as he elaborated:

I was happier. I was more up to do family stuff with the family, I set my goals differently, um, things like that, you know. I wanted to go out and get a job and help my wife get a job so we can pay the bills.

In choosing recovery, David also said that everything in his life changed. However, he noted that they had changed for the better:

It takes a little time to get adjusted to not having it, but once you do you feel a lot better, you can get jobs that's better and hold them down and just, just really unbelievable.

The men described the changes that occurred in their lives after making their final decision to stop abusing drugs and/or alcohol. In order to continue in recovery, participants had to sever ties with those who could influence them and cause them to relapse. Participants also spoke about avoiding places they had once frequented regularly while using. Some men even made the decision to leave their old lives behind and make geographical moves in order to help them in their recovery. Although the men described major adjustments in their lives, these adjustments ultimately helped them lead better lives in recovery.

Influences from Significant Others

Research (see Biernacki 1986; McIntosh and McKeganey 2002; Waldorf 1983) on the significance of others in recovery processes suggests that recovery from addiction is a phenomenon in which addicts must develop new relationships that help them forge new or residual roles that are circular to the processes of identity transformations. New activities and relationships are vital to the establishment of new identities. They supply former addicts with "identity materials"

(McIntosh and McKeganey 2002, p. 156) from which they can build and sustain new selves.

For example, when asked to talk about those who influenced them and helped them choose recovery, the majority of participants talked about the influence of family and friends. Several also talked about the positive influence of counselors and those they met in treatment. Martin talked about his best friend:

> Well, my best friend was probably my biggest advocate and he was the guy I was dealing with, he, he actually was supportive, he said if that's what you're going to do, do it.

Martin went on to say that in choosing recovery, he had lost several other friends. However, he felt that they had only associated with him because of "who I was and what I could do for them."

D talked about his sister and his best friend as being positive influences. "My sister's always been there and always supported anything and everything I've done." And his best friend was instrumental in probably "the first year to two years, of me being clean. He introduced me to the core group of friends I still run; hang around with to this day."

For Duane also, it was his father who was there to take him to his first meeting. Bobo talked about his wife and children influencing his decision to stop using. He also stated that while in long-term treatment, his counselor greatly influenced him:

> Just hearin' him talk, and hear him sharin' his experiences, and I'm like, wow, well, he's done way more time than I have, and he's used way more drugs than I have and he's older than me, so he's used it longer, and that's where that thing comes in, if he can do it, I can do it. I was like, okay, instead of goin' to visit, visit my family and my old friends and all that, instead of goin' to see them on the first day out, I'mma go to a meetin.'

Buck also described his counselor as playing an important part in his recovery. His counselor had done ten years in prison, was a recovering addict, and was a role model for Buck. For Buck, seeing that his counselor had once been to prison and was now successful allowed him to see that even though someone may have gone through difficult times in their lives, "things can get better."

Another participant, Blake, discussed a particular conversation he had with a former cellmate and the influence it had on his decision to stop using:

I was in prison, and I was, I got stuck with a cell mate, right off the bat, who was a recovering meth addict ... he was a year older than me, and looked about 20 years older than me ... he was losing his hair. What teeth he did have left in his head was black and rotted. He was having problems one night, and we got to talking and the one thing that always stuck in my head was, he said, "You don't wanna end up like me." That was the one thing that really set me off, was when he said that, and then you start thinking about that, and I didn't want to end up like him, I really didn't.

For Leonard, it was the mentoring that helped him in his recovery:

I was mentored ... by a group of old heroin addicts ... that are in rehab, and on the side, while I was living in _____ , I was spending tremendous amounts of time doing these long Socratic walks with guys who had been through the grist mill all their lives.

Although the men discussed different experiences in their lives, the majority noted that there were individuals in their lives who influenced their decision to stop using substances. Whether it was friends, family members or counselors, participants were nonetheless positively influenced by their significant others.

The Phasing Process of Change

For me the recovery program is a process and I guess you can call the steps, the steps help you work into phases that you may go through in recovery. They intertwine, you know, one phase locks into the next phase. Because you learn something from the first stage that you can apply in the second stage and then you learn something in that stage that you apply to the next stage, so it truly is a phasing process. (Bishop)

The previous section has provided a consideration of participants' awareness of their need to restructure alternative selves and social identities as they began their journeys into recovery. As participants became aware of alternative selves, identities began to change and as Bishop notes above, the process begins.

Recovery is "a process that requires some effort and invariably demands some form of behavioral plan for its successful completion" (Copeland 1998, p. 41). Further research (Brown 1985, p. 162) suggests that one of the most important changes that occur in recovery is the shift in "object attachment." The addict is primarily attached to their drug(s) of choice in addiction. In recovery, the individual needs to relinquish their drug(s) as a substance and an object of attachment. Substitution for the former use/abuse of controlled substances is a necessary component in recovery – something has to replace the addict's object of desire. Within AA and/or NA programs, such substitution may involve the organization itself, and/or individuals who are part of such programs.

When asked how they viewed their recovery, the majority of the men described recovery as an ongoing process. They also talked about different phases of recovery and explained that the phases meld into one another. One can learn something new in one phase and apply it in the next phase. Although the men described recovery as going through phases, the phases were hard to define. The phases were almost fluid and changed with each of the men.

Travis explained that he just stopped using, but described recovery as a long uphill process. He also noted that he continues to work on his recovery. Bobo described his recovery as an ongoing process. "It ain't never over! It just keeps goin'!" However, in the beginning, he admits that he did not understand the process and yet he was a part of it. Bobo noted that there is a "pre-stage" of recovery. While addicted, one may start to think about recovering. He had questioned himself asking: "Do I really wanna do this?"

JT described his recovery as a process and compared it to "a really long college course." He went on to explain that he learned through his experiences in recovery:

> You first start out; you're all happy about it and something new, something cool, and eventually its gets old and you wanna get away from it, but you can't, you kinda learn as you go. Eventually you get sick and tired of the whole, you know, going to work, so you wanna party again, and you get involved in it again, um, but you start losing everything, and realizing everything around you is falling apart so you wanna try to do better, you wanna get on the straight and narrow, and you try, and you have good days and bad days, and the bad days you fail, and then the good days you win.

David noted that he saw his recovery in specific phases. He explained that his relapses were phases in his recovery. He would go out and have a beer, and then find himself going to the bar which would then lead to drinking an entire gallon of alcohol. However, these relapses helped him learn and become stronger in his recovery.

Aaron also viewed his recovery in specific phases. He explained that he relapsed a few times and learned from those experiences, which helped him understand his urges. He described it as taking "two steps forward and one step back."

Two participants explained that recovery was an ongoing process and felt that there is no such thing as fully recovered. Blake stated:

> I don't think you're ever fully recovered. I think everyone is in recovery forever. I think once you have, once you've beat the drug, you'll forever be in recovery because, I don't think you can ever just say, okay I've been in NA for five years I'm done, I'm recovered, that's it I'm done! I've never heard that.

Duane also noted that he will always be a recovering alcoholic. However, he explained that he has recovered from the helpless, hopeless feelings associated with his addiction:

> I was not only hopeless; I was helpless, there wasn't anything that anybody that cared about me could do about it and the only thing I could seem to do about it. And the truth is I, I'm actually certain that I was granted some grace, it's just that simple, I was in a position where I was willing to accept a little bit of grace and God, I think it's always there, it's like the sunshine, it's just there all the time.

I asked the men how they would define their recovery: was it for them a matter of stages or a process? The participants explained that they viewed recovery as an ongoing process. Their argument for this view was that a stage began and ended but a process was something that moved back and forth, involving steps and decisions and a sequence of events. Some viewed their recovery in specific phases; however, these phases differed among the men. Some men viewed a relapse as a phase in recovery while others explained that one can recover without relapsing. The men explained that the phases meld into one another and lessons learned in one phase are useful in the next. All participants agreed that recovering from addiction is an ongoing lifelong process, one that never ends. According to them, every day is a new challenge – being an addict is something you never recover from, as it is part of their personality.

Programs for Change

As the following table shows, in making their final decision to stop abusing substances, the majority of participants (14) used certain programs and found them to be an important part of their recovery. These programs included AA, NA or other 12-step programs available to the men. Eleven participants stated that they did not use any programs as they processed their recovery.

Table 5.1. Types of Institutional and Community Support

Types of support	Frequency percent	(n)
AA/NA	16.0	(4)
AA	12.0	(3)
NA	16.0	(4)
Other	12.0	(3)
None	44.0	(11)
Total:	100.0	(25)

The 11 participants who did not use any institutional help stated that they found these organizations oppressive or not to their liking, or they stated that they did not need such support. For example, Buck had attended meetings in the past but admits that he just did not like it. Sterling also felt that the meetings were not for him and Trent felt that they had "no effect."

However, other participants did find such institutions helpful. For example, Bishop first began attending NA while incarcerated. "That's when I started going. I haven't used since the first day I went to NA." Bishop stated that NA saved his life.

Bobo attends AA and NA "about three times out of the week." He continued, explaining that for him the program is always helpful:

I'm gonna get somethin' out of it every time. That's my purpose of goin' in there, it's not where if I like the meetin' or I like the people, but the purpose of it is goin' there to get somethin' to keep me clean.

Another participant, Oreste, also attends AA three times a week and believes that it is a very good program for him. Oreste talked about the positive aspects of attending his AA meetings: "They've got a wonderful program in just helping you deal with life and, um, recognizing where you are weak, where you're strong and how to be honest."

Aaron continues to attend NA and AA meetings once a week as well, stating that it helps him in his everyday life because if he does not, "You're starting to repeat the steps to addiction all over again and eventually you end up right back at it."

Sherman goes to a 12-step program every day of the week. He continued, explaining that "I put something in my body everyday so I have to put recovery in my body everyday."

Duane had been a victim of sexual abuse and attended a trauma group and also continues to attend AA meetings. When speaking about his abuse Duane stated: "I was terribly ashamed of it and, um, what I, what I found out was that it didn't have anything to do with me." Duane finds the meetings very helpful and explained that for him: "The more that you talk about something the less power it has over you."

When asked if he had ever used a program to help him in his recovery, Kid explained that he is court ordered to go three times a week. But he does attend more meetings than he is ordered to attend and also speaks at seminars, part of his giving back to the community.

Blake began attending NA meetings while in prison. However, he did not find the meetings particularly helpful. The reason is:

I was surrounded by a bunch of guys who were there because the state said, "you're supposed to be here, this is where you need to be today." So, you have a bunch of guys who really don't care about getting better and they're in these classes because they have to be, not because they want to be, and if you were really serious about wanting to do what you're wanting to do, it's really hard to do when you're surrounded by that kind of atmosphere.

Blake also felt that the program was inadequate as it was run by individuals who were not former addicts. Although Blake did not like the NA group in prison, he was able to find a program he does enjoy and attends meetings weekly at his local church.

Some participants found that meetings and programs like AA and NA were not helpful. They had attended some in the past but did not feel it would benefit them. And some men simply did not like them. JT mentioned that he had attended a few meetings but felt confident enough in his recovery that he did not need to attend:

I understand it now to the point where I don't have to deal with it on a daily basis. I don't have to deal with it on a weekly basis. I think about it and I think it was stupid and it was dumb and I ain't going back there.

D does not attend meetings regularly but stated that he only does so if he is feeling really down or "really low." When asked how he is able to stay in recovery D responded that he had a very good support system to help him, including friends and his girlfriend.

Oliver explained how he felt about AA meetings:

·I'm not, I don't like being caged, pinned, tied down, and, uh, part of the thing I had with meetings that I've always had a problem with, and I tried going for a long time, but I was never successful and I used to hear people that would have 20 years sober, and I'd say, my God, if I hadn't of come to this meeting tonight I know I would have ended up drunk. I thought, my God, man, you, you haven't done anything, that thing has still got you. Your, your addiction has still got a hold of you, you are not in control of things, you know, and I believe in order to be sober or clean, you have to first want, want that, and then you have to somehow take the reins, you cannot rely on outside sources. You have to use this; you have to be in the driver's seat. God's here anyways, so you know, um, that is what rules my sobriety.

Oliver also admits that he has not used any program to help him in his recovery. When asked how he stays sober, Oliver explains that he has a good support system including his partner and his landlord who has 20 years of recovery.

There are some participants who found that AA and NA and other 12-step programs played very important roles in leading them into recovery. As Terry (2003) states, changing self-concepts are related to one's reference groups and one's interpretations of situations and events. So, too, recovering addicts will benefit by developing new relationships and self-concepts that either exclude or depreciate their old values (Terry 2003). Terry (2003) further argues that recovering addicts strongly identify with one another because of their shared problem – alcoholism and addiction – and their shared goal – sobriety or clean time. Some participants came to see AA and/or NA members as their family and they become "connected" to the group. Social support for self-change is related positively to the decision for changing oneself. Ebaugh (1988) suggests that another's approval can accelerate one's decision to change.

The majority of the men continue to attend such meetings and feel that they are beneficial in their recovery. Others found that such meetings were not helpful to them and simply did not like them. Each individual is different and thus they will choose different avenues to help them in their recovery. Nevertheless such programs were vital in the recovery process of several men.

Changing Friends/Changing Relationships

Stephens (1991) argues that one's recovery can only be accomplished through one's own efforts with assistance of others who have traveled the same pathways similar to many of the participants in this study. For example, when asked if their friendship networks were changing while going into recovery, the majority of the men explained that they had lost contact with many people. A small number of men were able to stay in contact with friends with whom they had once used as they continued to be supportive of their sobriety. Some men highlighted the fact that some individuals were not true friends and were simply around because of the drug and/or alcohol use. For example, Bobo stated that:

> Friends only want you around because you was a part of their gettin' high and gettin' drunk cycle ... you supply for them as well as they supply for you, so if you don't go around ... they're not gonna call you, or come lookin'for you, and while you gone to prison they done found someone to replace you anyway, so it was an easy step.

Bobo noted that it was an easy process to sever ties with friends with whom he had once used. He began making new friends and now has many close friends whom he met while attending AA and NA.

Herb also lost contact with many individuals whom he had once considered his friends:

> I considered the ones I (used) with as acquaintances, now, because when I stopped using, they just disappeared. I didn't have to call them and tell them don't come around. Trust was an issue with me because all of my so-called friends who just disappeared, now I'm saying, okay, what kind of friend is a friend, I mean ... I didn't know what a friend was, that kinda shocked me, I said here I am 40-something years old and I don't even know what word—what is a true friend.

Sterling felt that he was finally able to see who his "real friends were." He went on to say:

> Most of 'em, the people that I had been close to ever since, you know, junior high or even grade school, I found out they weren't real friends at all, so new friends, a lot of new—a few of the old ones, but far less friends than I used to have, but the ones I have, I know are real friends so it doesn't really matter, it's better in the end.

Blake also discussed losing contact with people in his life and not having the same friends as he did before. Blake had to make changes in order to keep his sobriety. He explains that he is now good friends with his ex-wife who helped him get in contact with a group to support him in his recovery. Buck noted that he also changed his friends. However, he explained that his situation can be difficult at times: "There's friends you can change and friends you can't. I can't change family members, you know." Although Buck was able to cut ties with user friends, his family continues to use. Despite his family using around him, Buck is able to keep his sobriety.

> Everybody sitting around me drinking for Thanksgiving, and I'll just, I'll cook the whole dinner myself, you know, when everybody else gets drunk because that keeps me occupied, I'm doing something else, you know.

Another participant, Aaron, explained that when he was released from prison he never returned to his old neighborhood. Aaron made new friends in recovery stating: "I have people who are recovering addicts or alcoholics that are my friends, they know the struggles that we go through every day and [are] able to lend a helping shoulder."

Trent had remained close to a few friends he had known since early adolescence:

> A few of them are the same; they're just old school friends, you know, that had been friends, and through this part of my life with me too so, you know, we're friends for life but, yeah, I've slowly been making new friends too. I had basically two groups of friends; I have a group of friends from the drug days who I still love and are still my lifelong friends because we share so much, and we get along so well. But then I have this complete other circle that I've started making.

Although they are friends with whom he had once used, Trent is able to stay close to them, while also making new friends in recovery.

Although the men described losing many friends when they chose recovery, they saw this as a positive experience which allowed them to see their "true friends." The majority found support and friendship among other recovering addicts. For some, like Buck, it can be difficult to continue in recovery when one's family continues to use. However, in continuing to stay positive and persevering, Buck is able to maintain his sobriety.

Often, when addicts are using they are surrounded by a community of users. In choosing recovery, obviously one must often remove themselves from such an environment. Waldorf (1983), Biernacki (1986) and McIntosh and McKeganey (2002) also suggest that recovery from addiction is a phenomenon in which addicts must develop new relationships that help them forge new or residual roles that are circular to the processes of identity transformations.

Relapse as a Learning Experience

Relapse can be defined as a discrete event, which occurs at the moment a person resumes drug use, or as a process which occurs over time. In the latter view, it may mean resumption of addiction; return to drug use of the same intensity as in the past; daily drug use for a specified number of sequential days (e.g., daily use for one week); or a consequence of the drug use, such as the return to the hospital for further drug abuse treatment (Litman, Stapleton, Oppenheim, Peleg and Jackson 1983; Tims and Leukefeld 1986). For some participants in this study relapse was a regular occurrence. Prochaska, Norcross and DiClemente (1994, p. 48) argue that such "recycling" gives individuals who are former addicts opportunities to learn. Prochaska et al. (1994, p. 48) refer to the term, "recycle to relapse" and argue that actions followed by relapses are far better than no actions at all. Table 5.2 highlights the number of relapses participants experienced.

Table 5.2. Participants' Relapses

No. of relapses	Frequency percent	(n)
0	28.0	(7)
1	44.0	(11)
2–3	28.0	(7)
Total:	100.0	(25)

When asked if they had ever relapsed, seven participants stated that they had never done so, while 11 men had relapsed once. Seven participants had relapsed from two to three times during their recovery. For example, Blake admitted that he had thought about using again, but noted that he had never relapsed. When asked what kept him from relapsing, Blake explained:

I have a notebook, just a little book that's, like the composition books that they use, it's a little itty bitty one, and the days that I wake up and I don't feel myself or I don't feel, I wouldn't say good about myself, I just don't feel right, I will wake up, and I will write what's good in my life, and write that down. And I date it, and I write what the positive is, and if I ever have any doubts the rest of the day, I go back to the page that I just wrote, the last page that I wrote, I look at that, I look at the positives. My kids, if you look through every day, that'd be the first on the list, is my kids.

Bobo stated that he has things in his life that are worth more than any highs. "I found somethin' more valuable than that high and I'm not gonna, I don't wanna give it up, I'm not gonna give it up." When asked if he had ever taken a step back in his recovery, Leonard responded, "No, never, not once."

Herb had never relapsed either and talked about his experience:

Some people say and even in the literature that some people need to relapse to really get a grip and to feel the pain and so forth and so on and I see people come back in after relapsing and I see the pain and embarrassment on their face and, and I'm like wow, I just don't, I don't want to pick up another white key tag [the first key you receive in NA].

Sherman stated that he had never relapsed. When asked why not, he responded:

Honestly, I don't know, I've been in situations where, uh, I should have … or back in the day I would have used, but, but honestly I just look at the light, usings not a option for me today, I don't have to use to feel. I don't have to use to face nothing now.

Bishop also stated that he had never relapsed since entering recovery. He explained how he views relapse:

And a lot of people say that relapse is necessary or a part of recovery, maybe for some, they may have to relapse in order to really, really get it together. Our program says that many times in relapse brings about a more serious application to the program. For some people it's true, it doesn't have to happen, you don't have to use again ever. And that's my message – to other recovering people you *don't* [emphasis added] have to use again, ever, it's a choice.

Bishop further explained that he is very aware of the consequences if he were to use again, such as he could "be in the penitentiary in the next four, five, six years, maybe in the next day or two." He also explained that when it comes to recovery that it is different for each person and those who do not succeed are the ones who stop doing the things they need to stay clean.

Other participants such as Oreste and Travis also stated that they had never relapsed. Martin had also never relapsed and explained:

> I don't have that desire inside to use again, I just, I guess it's a mental thing. It's that dependence you know, and the physical aspect isn't there.

There were participants who highlighted the fact that they had not relapsed since entering recovery. However, there were several men who admitted that they had relapsed at one time or another in their recovery. They explained that there were different reasons that led them to use again. For example, Gorilla explained that he had relapsed once before moving away from the area in which he had been an active user. Nick had also relapsed once. He stated that:

> The second time after I got out of treatment the first time I relapsed again. And after the second time I just gave it up. That was it. And I never used no more.

Rock admitted that he had relapsed on one occasion after going into recovery. When asked how that happened, Rock explained that it all began when he talked to an old friend:

> You know, I was actively involved with NA, I was going to meetings on a regular basis, got a sponsor, workin' the steps, but I was doin' other things that they suggested for me to do. One of the guys that I knew that was in prison with me, he was a heroin addict ... he asked me, "Could I talk to you for a minute?" he pulled me over to the side, and he asked me if I could bring him some heroin you know, so I said, no man, you don't want to do that, you're going into recovery, but in the back of my mind, I thought I might be able to do this.

Rock conceded that although he had not yet begun using, the act of going to get drugs and selling them, to him, felt that he had already relapsed mentally.

Buck stated that a relapse is a learning experience where one can acknowledge the relapse, understand why it happened, and learn to prevent it from happening again. When asked what caused him to relapse, Buck noted that family and financial stress were key triggers that led him to start using again. Buck explained that he saw relapse as a normal part of recovery and described his experiences:

> Sometimes I'd go two and half years without using, use again for six months, stop, you know, for six months, use again, and sometimes the periods would be shorter, relapse again for a few weeks, and then stop. That's one of the biggest mistakes I think people make about recovery: "I relapsed, oh no, it's over now, my clean time's shot." Man you gotta get back on the horse, if you relapse, you know, okay, you know, you recognize what's happened, why it happened, and then start over.

He went on to say that he has spoken to people who do not understand that relapse can be a normal part of recovery. He noted also that the judicial system certainly does not understand that. He further explained that a person can learn from their experiences and try to prevent another relapse.

Aaron stated that he had relapsed three times. He did not continue using because a friend discovered he had used and convinced him to stop. The last time he relapsed, his wife found out he had used again and she gave him an ultimatum: "You either have to make a choice, me, or the drugs." This certainly was a motivator in his stopping using substances for good.

Sterling also relapsed after he had gone into recovery. He described his experience that triggered his relapse:

> I did have a few beers on, um, the 4th of July and then it kinda set me over the edge, you know, I wanted to, to drink again and then like a few nights later I went out and drank all night, got really drunk and sick and then 'bout a couple months later I did it again, and then after that second time, after throwing up both times really bad, I just lost it, I said, you know, I'm sick of waking up and throwing up and having that horrible headache and that was just enough for me.

As a result of that experience, he believed that he became stronger in his recovery.

There were two participants who noted that they still continued to drink. Timex explained that he continues to drink occasionally. When asked if he had ever relapsed D responded: "In some people's opinion, yeah." When asked to discuss what he meant, he explained:

> On occasion I will have a drink. I might have a glass of wine with dinner, yeah, but I don't really consider my drinking being a problem. I've never considered drinking to be one of my problems. I can go out to dinner, sit down, drink a beer, or have a glass of wine, and leave the restaurant and that's all I drink, it's not a problem.

Although Timex and D continue to use alcohol they stated that they feel comfortable in their recovery and felt that alcohol was not a problem in their lives.

There were several participants who did not relapse once they had entered recovery. They described different experiences that helped them be successful in their recovery. The men explained that they had found something in their lives that was worth more than any high. There were, however, several participants who discussed relapse. The men described different triggers that caused them to use again. Yet, with their strength and the help of others, they were able to once again go into recovery and continue to strive to be abstinent, thus attempting to stabilize their recovery.

Stabilizing Recovery

Biernacki (1986, p. 25) states that

> Recovery refers to the process through which a new calculus or arrangement of identities and perspectives emerges and becomes relatively stabilized. This process entails a different articulation of identities in which the identity as an addict becomes de-emphasized (both symbolically and socially) relative to other identities existing or emerging as part of the person's overall life arrangement.

As highlighted in the above quote, participants talked about how their lives, as well as how their individual selves and identities had changed as they stabilized recovery processes. When first entering recovery, participants described doing different things in their lives. They had once been consumed by drugs and/or alcohol but were now able to engage in different activities. As White (2007, p. 236) argues:

> Recovery is the experience (a process and a sustained status) through which individuals, families, and communities impacted by severe alcohol and other drug (AOD) problems utilize internal and external resources to voluntarily resolve these problems, heal the wounds inflicted by AOD-related problems, actively manage their continued vulnerability to such problems, and develop a healthy, productive, and meaningful life.

Former addicts have often described their drug of choice as their companion or best friend in life. When using, addicts are often immersed in a drug and/or alcohol culture, where their lives revolve around such substances. Their thoughts are consumed with determining how they will get money and how they will get their next high. Often, when entering recovery, individuals will have to find something to replace their drug of choice. When interviewed, the men described different activities they were now engaged in which included spending time with family and friends, and engaging in different activities such as helping out in AA and/or NA, and doing their hobbies once again.

When asked what took the place of drugs and/or alcohol in their lives, six men talked about spending time with their family and friends. Ebaugh (1988) argues that the influence of families, children and/or partners relates to the importance of "bridging" (Ebaugh 1988, p. 147) among former addicts. Such "bridging" (Ebaugh 1988, p. 147) incorporates the process of reestablishing relationships with friends, family, hobbies, or jobs. People with bridges establish new identities and new roles as nonaddicts more easily (Ebaugh 1988; Granfield and Cloud 1999, Stephens 1991; Snow 1997). "Bridging" (Ebaugh 1988, p. 147) involves a connection to others, thus allowing the person to see himself as part of the larger whole once again. For example, JT and David commented that their wives replaced their drug and/or alcohol use. Kid noted that he spent a lot of time with his daughter, doing all kinds of "things" with her such as attending the local fair. Buck also spends much more time with his daughter, explaining that they "kind of get along better than we ever did before." For Daved and Nick, it was their families as well. Nick talked also about simply engaging in different activities:

> I mean really it's just sporting events or some type of event, playing basketball, or playing cards, stuff like that and being around people that are clean.

Other participants became actively involved in AA and NA. What took the place of drugs for Rock was "going to meetings and bein' actively involved in my program." Rock also talked about helping others and speaking at different meetings, including returning to the prison where he had once been incarcerated:

> I do speaker meets in different places, and I'm really involved with giving back, you know. By giving back, going to the jails, letting people … seeing that "hey man," it is possible you can change.

Sherman also began "going to meetings and hanging with my sponsor and people within the program." He also continues to spend a lot of his time reading. D noted that in the beginning, he had to catch up on a lot of sleep. He admitted that using methamphetamines caused him to stay up for days. At first, what took the place of his drug use was simply sleeping for days on end. He went on to say that he then began attending meetings:

> I would say meetings were really instrumental when I first got clean. Sometimes it's nice to sit there and listen, and know that I'm not the only person that goes through what I have to go through all the time.

For example, when Martin began his recovery he took up new hobbies. He stated:

> I finally figured out you could have fun without substances, so when I figured that out I took up hobbies. I played the drums, I was in the band at that point, the marching band, and I played on the drum line. When I would get mad or frustrated there's nothing better than hitting things with a stick so playing the drums was great. I took up hobbies like, um, disc golfing. I started playing video games a lot.

Harvey talked about attending different auctions, which he enjoyed. Travis explained that while using he enjoyed working on different models and putting them together; now in recovery he wanted to continue this type of hobby.

Sterling noted that it was difficult for him in the beginning to try and do the things he used to:

> I didn't paint or draw a single thing for like the first 18 months—a little over a year to 18 months I just, I had no desire to do the things I used to do, and I used to play guitar, bass and drums, and I can't do that anymore.

After suffering a stroke he did not have the ability to use both hands. However, Sterling gradually started painting again.

Oliver talked about his desire to help others and working with addicts. He also took up a hobby working with leather and doing Native American art crafts. In his recovery, Duane also became more involved in activities he had enjoyed when he was younger, such as hobbies and fishing.

As this section has highlighted, when first entering recovery, many of the participants who had once been consumed by drugs and/or alcohol were now able to engage in different activities; activities which now were giving them some stability in their lives. Other stable behaviors for these men included work and school as the following section emphasizes.

Work and School

Much of a person's ability to extract himself/herself from substance misuse is related to the range of perceptible and imperceptible resources available to that individual (Cloud and Granfield 2008). Many of my participants reengaged in institutional life, such as work and school often within the institutions to which they had been connected. For example, several participants began to spend their time working or continuing their education. Several participants talked about their current employment as something that keeps them on track in their recovery. It was important for them to stay employed and some of the men really enjoyed their new jobs. For example, Buck stated: "When I got out of prison last time, I started working for a big company that frames apartment buildings and hotels, and large commercial construction, and I worked for them for two years." Buck and three other employees from the company then decided to start their very own company, a cooking business.

Travis replaced his drug use with work, whereby he "worked all the time." For Bishop, having a job changed everything as he states:

> I had a job when I got out of prison. I didn't have to go look for a job. And that was a big stumbling block for me was to go look for a job. I already was self-defeating by saying that nobody was going to hire me because I've got this long record and I don't have a work history. And that was the reality of course.

Trent began attending school again, however, this time it was different:

> I came back home from the navy and my parents were like, "We'll pay for you to go to school, but, you know, you have to focus on it," and ... once again it was kind of like I'm doing this more to appease you as my parents. But in the past year or two year, I, it's come full circle to me, that I'm not doing this for them, I need to get on the ball and do this for myself.

Aaron, David and Bobo all started working in new positions. D began working as a bartender but eventually moved on to waiting tables. Another participant, Duane, was proud that he was self-employed working in construction.

For two men, religion took the place of the drugs and/or alcohol in their lives. Leonard talked about his spirituality and noted "I went from a ... a taker to a giver." Sterling also turned to religion and began reading various religious materials.

Some participants admitted that they may have switched one addiction for another, but to less harmful ones. Bobo and Martin replaced their substance use with soda, Aaron with cigarettes and coffee. Martin explained that he attributes his addiction to soda to "my addictive personality, I'm jumping from thing to thing, I don't know, trying to still replace it." However, he finds that "overall, I think I just replaced it with peace, this, this thing inside of me that just says you're done."

Participants had once been immersed in their drug and/or alcohol use. Their time had been consumed by their need to use and, being in recovery, the men had to find new ways to spend their time. Whether it was their new jobs, schoolwork, spending time with their families or engaging in activities they had once enjoyed, the men were able to find new things to take the place of the substances that they had once used.

McIntosh and McKeganey (2002) argue that new activities and relationships are vital to the establishment of new identities as the participants in this study also stated. Such activities and relationships supply former addicts with "identity materials" (McIntosh and McKeganey 2002, p. 156) from which they can build and sustain new selves. Recovery can be understood as an ongoing process of interaction through which people adopt new meanings and new self-images (Granfield and Cloud 1999). As stated earlier, it is also "a process that requires some effort and invariably demands some form of behavioral plan for its successful completion" (Copeland 1998, p. 41).

Future Plans in Recovery

> I would like to be, to settle down and retire as a drug counselor. I would like to either manage or own a lot of ... treatment houses ... mainly for people that's comin' out of prison that don't know how to live ... and keep supportin' my family and just live. (Bobo)

As Bobo states above, many of the participants, when asked to describe their plans for the near and far future, spoke positively about looking forward to their future. Several participants talked about getting back on their feet and finding stable employment. Others looked forward to owning their own homes and supporting their families. Several participants noted that they planned on going back to school. There were also several men who spoke about helping others. They discussed their interest in helping former addicts and some men stated that they would like the opportunity to become substance abuse counselors.

David noted that for him the plan is simply "to get a full time job to keep and get a home and take care of my wife and live better than I had been." Travis hopes to be successful and own his own company; he is putting money aside in order to obtain a license so he can start building privacy fences.

Gorilla stated that he would like to find employment in order to have a stable income. He also explained that he would like to get a degree in criminology in order to become a parole officer, a job that he felt he would be successful at as he has had experiences with his own parole officers.

When asked to describe his plans for the near and far future, Aaron responded:

> Get back on my feet again, after losing everything I had, you know, starting all over again ... getting a job, or staying with a job. Roof over your head, food to eat, someplace to lay your head and sleep.

Aaron commented that his long term goal is to continue his sobriety, go to college, and work with people.

When asked about their near and future plans, there were several participants who discussed their desire to return to school. Some participants explained that they would like to go back to school in order to have more opportunities to help others. Martin explained:

> I wanna get my degree ... I wanna have a business, and have it going so well that I actually don't have to work unless I want to, and I wanna go to foreign countries ... specifically India and, uh, build schools ... different things like that and help the children that no one wants, uh, because my wife's father is from there and they tell me stories all the time of, of, um, kids just abandoned, uh, living in the city dumps and all this stuff and I wanna build orphanages and schools and educate 'em and, you know.

D stated his future plans:

> I was gonna go to full-time grad school, but, now that I have a child on the way, I'm hoping that I can get a decent, like a decent government job, either working with high-risk adolescents ... like a juvenile officer, or a substance abuse counselor, during the day, and then part-time.

Bishop stated that he hopes to go back to school and get his bachelor's degree. He explained that he would also like to help expand a program that helps substance abusers. This expansion would include transitional housing to help them ease back into society.

Along with Bishop's idea, there were other participants who discussed the fact that they would like to help others who were also suffering from addiction. Oliver noted that in the near and far future he would like to own his own home and possibly go into counseling. He explained:

> I hope to be able to, uh, get into counseling, uh, hopefully ... I would still like to be able to build a house, uh, you know, in the woods somewhere, uh, small chalet. Just to have my own place, and that when I, when I do leave this world, that I leave something behind besides bad memories ... memories of addiction, and, uh, just a ragged life, you know ... I want the people that I leave behind to be taken care of, and I hope to be able to get to a point where I'm able to do that before I leave here, you know.

For JT, his future was family and a new baby. Buck looked forward to being financially stable and hopes to be able to take care of his wife and family as well. Buck also hopes to continue in his recovery and noted that in order to do so he must stay in the routine he has developed:

> For me to stay in recovery I have to always keep on it, you know, I can't stop going to Bible study, or doing the things that works for me to keep me sober. Once I stop doing that, I'll relapse again, I'll get off the routine that I got.

When asked about his plans for the near and far future, Kid stated that he hopes for continuing sobriety, and "a successful, normal life." Blake noted that he would like to make amends with his parents:

> My near future is, once I get my job back, is I am going to move out of my parent's house. I think part of my recovery process, not just so much as to stay off the drugs, as I want to do what I can to make amends for the shit that I did earlier and part of that is paying my parents back. I mean, whether I could give them back anything, or, you know ... for them, in their eyes, that's me trying to help to do what I can, that I'm making an effort to make amends for the things that I did. And I think that's more of what they want to see than, than what the dollar amount is. I think that they know I am trying, so.

For Herb, his future was complicated:

The future is just having time for my babies, you know, I don't even have my life insurance or anything, or any kind of education, uh, fun, college fun or anything, so I really need to, uh, get serious about that area of my life, cuz it's just been so raggedy for so long. Down the road that's what I'm building to, is to have something as far as that integrity as a man for my family and, you know, that legacy, and not just leave my daughters with a bunch of trucks and trailers and, you know, just mentally, emotionally, and physically, have something sound. There was no balance, so I have to learn balance too, you know.

Many of the men spoke positively about the days to come. Several participants noted that they hoped to find long-term employment and become financially stable. They expressed their desire to finally be able to provide for their families. Several participants also discussed their plans to return to school and further their education. There were several men who aspired to help others suffering from addiction. Some of the men wanted to work to expand programs in their area while others talked about receiving training in order to become substance abuse counselors

The foregoing discussion from participants in this study illustrates what various scholars (Brudenell 1997; Denzin 1987a, b; Haas 2003; Van den Bergh 1991) argue: recovery is a process that occurs over time and involves psychological, physical, cognitive, emotional, and spiritual changes. These processes involve both internal and external changes; they are continuous processes that do not take place in a vacuum (Abbott 1995; Denzin 1987b; Underhill 1991) and involve conscious changes in individuals' life directions (Smith 1991).

Summary

This chapter has highlighted men's relevant experiences while addicted. An exploration of participants' recovery experiences through a consideration of shifting self-images as they chose new identities and a sense of new selves for their lives was offered. Major adjustment in participants' lives were enabled through influences from their significant others as well as programs they chose in recovery. Relapse was a challenge that the men in many cases were still struggling with as they stabilized their recovery processes along with work and school. Future plans were significant among most participants as they worked to cement their recovery processes.

In the following chapter, I first offer a short discussion of the study. Following this overview, I conclude with an overview of participants' opinions and insights into various aspects of their addiction and recovery processes along with their suggestions for change for other individuals who may be thinking of recovery. Finally, I offer my suggestions for changes in policies in the field of men's addiction and recovery processes.

6

Lessons Learned

In the preceding chapters, I explored men's perspectives of how they began to engage with addiction to drugs and/or alcohol, how they processed addiction experiences, and how they disengaged from their use of substances. I employed a qualitative method coupled with the paradigm of symbolic interaction for this research. The qualitative method enabled me to understand the meanings that the men I interviewed attached to events, situations, and actions, including the accounts that they gave of their lives and their experiences.

Of primary interest in this research were men's definitions of addiction and recovery and their interpretations of how they made meanings of such experiences, as previous chapters have shown. I hope in this study that I have helped as Walker (1985, p. 22) argues, "To understand and demystify drug taking, dispel unhelpful myths and stereotypes about drug users, build and develop theories of addiction and formulate and evaluate drug policy and practice."

I begin this chapter with a short discussion of the study followed by various indicators of participants' insights into their feelings about substances now that they are in recovery. In other words, I give my participants the "last word" on the topic of addiction and recovery for them. Following these insights thoughts on their achievements as they recovered are documented. I also offer their ideas of what recovery means to them and also what factors need to be in place for men to enter recovery including the following: individual decisions for change, the importance of a support system, and the importance of realizing that recovery is a lifelong process. Further, participants' insights into their opinions of the differences between their use/abuse of substances and that of women are offered. Finally, I conclude with participants' suggestions for change for other individuals who may be thinking of recovery coupled with my suggestions for changes in policies in the field of men's addiction and recovery processes.

Discussion

The previous chapters show that the experiences of the men as they narrated their experiences of addiction and recovery are replicated in much of the literature on such processes for them. However, my findings not only give a "voice" to the men in their narrations but also help to extend the knowledge in the field of addiction and recovery. My participants' narratives help to reinforce current thinking in the area of addiction and recovery for men.

Even though I cannot attempt to generalize the findings from this research to the wider population of men who have experienced addiction and recovery processes, this study has provided "a form of systematic empirical inquiry into meaning" (Shank 2002, p. 5) for a small number of individuals. Denzin and Lincoln (2000) argue that qualitative research involves an interpretive and naturalistic approach: "This means that qualitative researchers study things in their natural settings, attempting to make sense of, or to interpret, phenomena in terms of the meanings people bring to them" (Denzin and Lincoln 2000, p. 3). I have used an approach to inquiry that stands on its own and that allowed me as the researcher to attain a glimpse of my participants' worlds. I argue that this approach is important as it enabled the men I interviewed to offer their perspectives on their experiences, a valid and significant undertaking within the field of addiction and recovery.

In the following section, I highlight participants' thoughts on how they feel towards their drug(s) of choice now while in their recovery.

Feelings about Controlled Substances While in Recovery

When asked how they now felt about controlled substances the men described very different feelings toward them. Some of the participants explained that they missed the alcohol and/or drugs and missed the feeling they felt when they were using. Some men felt neutral and just saw drugs as something that was once part of their lives. Others explained that they continued to have positive feelings toward drugs but understand that they can no longer use. Other men described having very negative feelings about controlled substances and saw them as their "enemy."

Kid admitted that although he is in recovery:

There's lots of parts I miss ... I had good times, some good times drinkin' ... I dated a lot of women ... a lot of different women. It made me feel like that I ... was somebody ... like I fit into the crowd.

Buck also talked about missing the feeling he got from using and understands that in order to be vigilant in recovery, he has to stay away from alcohol and drugs.

A few men noted that they now had neutral feelings towards controlled substances. Daved explained: "I can look at it and see that it caused a lot of problems in my life but I don't think that's an enemy I think it was just part of my disease." He continued to elaborate on his view: "I always looked at it like a medicine, this is my medicine, this is not my friend or so forth and so on, it's my medicine."

Herb stated:

> It was my best friend, but, uh, I really have no feelings towards it now, I, I despise what it did to me, you know. But I also have to have respect for it, also to know what it can do, not only to me but to others around me and so forth, and seeing what it's still doing to addicts out there, you know. Its, it's a, it's a big powerful weapon that the demon used and he uses it, he gets in your mind, he uses that to destroy, but that's his job, his job is out to destroy and, uh, once he can get that seed planted in your head, that's what he does.

Sherman also did not have any positive or negative feelings towards controlled substances. He saw them as "Something that controlled my life for years and I know that it doesn't have to control my life anymore, no one is in control of my life but me."

Often, addicts will talk about their past drug use and describe their drug of choice as a friend, their best friend. Once they have entered recovery, they can continue to see controlled substances as a friend or begin to see them as the enemy. When he was using, Nick saw cocaine as a friend. Although Nick suffered through addiction he continues to see cocaine as "a friend but I can't use it. Marijuana, ah, it's the same thing, it's still a friend, but I can't use it."

Duane explained: "There's not any doubt that they saved my life, I would have killed myself long ago … I don't, I don't have anything against alcohol or drugs." Although Duane's addiction to methamphetamines had caused problems in his life, he feels that they "were a great solution; they worked for a long time." He explained that without the escape he got from using drugs, he would have ended his life long ago.

Sterling also does not have anything against alcohol and/or drugs. "I really don't think alcohol is that bad unless you, unless it, um, you let take control of your life." Sterling also sees drugs as "just something to do to get high and have a good time."

When asked how he now felt about controlled substances, Bishop responded:

> If drugs were sitting on the table, I have a choice. I can be talking to you and I can get up and go about my business or I can say can I have a little bit of that. So that's a choice I have today. Many times in addiction we lose control of our choices from day-to-day. And a lot of people don't identify with that – but that's exactly what happens, you lose the ability to make sound decisions from one minute to the next because it's all based on your disease of addiction.

Although Bishop explained that drugs are just drugs, he admits "I don't like them. I don't like to see people doing them 'cause I know what it leads to."

Some men described that they now had neutral feelings about alcohol and/or drugs. Others explained that they had nothing against controlled substances. However, for some men, when asked how they now felt about controlled substances, several men described very negative feelings. Some participants referred to them as "the enemy."

Martin noted that "for a long time after I saw it as a friend." He went on to say that he now sees them as the enemy. JT also described methamphetamines as "A drug from hell. It's not a friend, it's the worst enemy." Trent also felt that methamphetamines are his worst enemy. Trent feels so strongly about the negative impacts of methamphetamines that he tries to convince others not to use:

> I'd turn anybody that I felt like I had influence over away from it, you know, I'd tell them my story and tell them what it's like, what it's really like after you look back on it and keeping them away from it, like that kinda be like the mentor, you know, if I see somebody trying to do it, or trying to fall into it, I try to stop 'em before they actually fall down because once you fall down into that addiction, it's really difficult.

Rock described very negative feelings about heroin and expressed concern and anger about changes in the production of heroin which makes the drug much more dangerous. "Right now I feel real angry about it because today they got something, I don't know what they are doing with the heroin or what they are cutting it with but it's killing people." When asked how he felt about controlled substances he stated that he felt "nothing, it is the enemy." He expanded:

> It is the enemy, yeah, because I know that it's kinda like the God and the devil, God's will is for you to do the right thing, the devil's will is

trying to destroy you, any shape, form or fashion that he can, so that's what I look at – whether it be alcohol, marijuana or crack, any kind of drug, I look at it in league with the devil and I know what his job is, it's to destroy my life if I let it, that's his purpose, you know.

Travis stated: "I don't like it … I would not go back to it for nothin'." He explained that he does not want to go back to where he was before. Where every day meant he had to think,

Okay, I got to deal this many drugs so I can pay for my attorney to get out of this trouble so I can turn around and get caught doing the drugs, to have to buy another attorney, you know, ah, I don't want that.

Two participants, David and Bobo, explained that they could no longer stand the smell of alcohol and felt sick to their stomach if they did smell it.

Although all the men suffered from addiction, they described having different feelings about controlled substances. Some men described having neutral feelings about controlled substances. Some participants felt very positively about alcohol and/or drugs, and one participant even felt that drugs had saved his life. However, for others, controlled substances represented a very dark time in their lives and several men referred to controlled substances as their enemy.

What did the participants see as their greatest achievements now while in recovery? The following section highlights their answers.

Greatest Achievements

When asked to consider their greatest achievement in life, participants discussed their children, their academic achievements and other things they had accomplished. Although all the participants had suffered through addiction, only four men felt that their sobriety had been their greatest achievement. Other participants discussed their own personal accomplishments. The majority of the men felt that their greatest achievement in life was their children and being able to support them. For example, when asked to consider the greatest achievement in his life so far, Blake talked about his children. He discussed his ability to provide for his children and give them the opportunities that he did not have growing up:

I think that the greatest achievement is watching my kids grow up and not end up like I did … all my kids have really good grades. But I think probably my biggest achievement is just watching my kids grow up … they have the better, I guess better resources than I did when I was growing up. They are on a track to not do what I did.

Buck also discussed his children. For Buck, his greatest achievement is "raising them three kids, and, my oldest daughter, she doesn't even use drugs, alcohol, cigarettes, or nothing, and raising those kids and keeping them alive through all this, so that's my greatest achievement I guess." For Aaron, his greatest achievement was also his son.

Kid referred to his children as "gifts":

The most significant thing that has ever happened to me is the five gifts I've gotten through … my children … my five gifts of life with my children. My children are the most significant, significant thing in my life right now, and, will ever be. I've got a lot to be grateful for, you know. Every night, I thank God for all the good things He's given me … and also pray to not get in front of Him, or behind Him, but just stay right there beside Him.

For Gorilla, the greatest achievement in his life was "being a good father." Bobo stated that it was "being able to take care of me and my family and to maintain the responsibilities that I have. They were my responsibility that I neglected in the past, so I gotta clean all that up."

Travis, Leonard and Daved also noted that their children were the most important things in their lives. For Oreste, his achievement was his sons. He stated:

I am very proud of my sons and I consider that to be an achievement that I am at least partly responsible for and I have a wife who feels loved.

There were only four participants who felt that their sobriety was the greatest achievement in their lives. Oliver stated that

My greatest achievement is getting sober, and my sobriety. I can't think of anything that I'm more proud of or that means more to me than being able to realize sobriety.

Oliver further explained that for him, it is not just about being able to say "I'm sober, you know today. I didn't drink today." But rather, the amazing thing is that he is able to say "I don't drink." Oliver explained that "being able to say that is, is a huge thing in my life, very, very big."

David stated that: "My achievement was the day I woke up and said never again, not even the beer, nothing. I'm very proud. To do that and not even do a rehab or anything." JT explained that his "greatest achievement is getting probably married, and getting my life turned around away from drugs." Trent noted that his greatest achievement was "getting myself off of meth."

Bishop talked about how important "giving back" was to him in the prison where he was once incarcerated as he stated:

> My greatest achievement I think is working in the same facility, the prison facility that I came home from. I've gone back to do good. The director of the program … she came on long after I had left there but I always stayed in touch with the program and she called me and asked me how I would feel about working as a substance abuse counselor. It is a unique experience for one to have been incarcerated in a particular prison, and then have the opportunity to go back to that same prison to work and help others.

For Sterling, his greatest achievement was getting his book published. Rock talked about becoming an entrepreneur and owning his own clothing store. He explained that he had turned his life around and turned something negative into something positive.

D highlighted the fact that he will graduate with honors from college. He continued:

> Coming from what I came from. You know, I mean, you know, five and a half, six years ago, I was cooking and slinging dope, putting a needle in my arm, and now I'm getting ready to graduate, you know.

Another participant, Harvey, noted that his greatest achievement is that he will often help those in a similar situation he once found himself in:

> I always try helping people; you know what I'm sayin'? Just, when someone needs help I try and give it to them the best I can. I'll help people out with a place to stay, maybe, or a ride somewhere or whatever, you know.

Although the men were very proud of being in recovery, only four participants felt that their sobriety was their greatest achievement in life. For many, their children are the most important part of their lives and their children are what they are most proud of. Other participants listed personal accomplishments like owning their own business and their academic success. Several of the men also made note of the fact that they were very proud of their abilities to help others.

How does one make the decision to change from addiction to one's recovery? I asked the participants for their insights into this issue as documented in the following section.

Individual Decisions for Change

A few of the participants offered their view that the decision to change one's use of substances must be an individual one. For example, Oliver noted that:

> You have to be at a point in your life where you're sick and tired of being sick and tired. I think the biggest obstacle for most people that are addicted is like I said … they've conditioned themselves to accept things as they are.

Oliver also explained that a person must decide that they want more out of life and make an individual decision to stop using. Sterling reiterated Oliver's comments when he stated: "They need to have in their mind that they are gonna change; you can't force anybody to do anything."

Three participants felt that two specific factors need to be in place for individuals to quit, including "hitting rock bottom," and becoming "tired" of the lifestyle of using. For example, Rock commented that he needed to hit rock bottom before he could go into recovery:

> My bottom was when I used drugs, I commit crimes, when I commit crimes, I go to jail, I got tired of going to jail.

He noted that everyone has a "rock bottom," but they have to find it, and some people find it in a short period of time, and for some people it may take the rest of their lives. JT also felt that:

> It really depends on them. You got to make up your own mind if you want to stop; if you don't want to stop you're not going to. You just gotta have, finally have an epiphany, something gotta click in your brain and say that's enough, I'm tired of this.

Not only must individuals be ready to change from addiction to recovery, but also there needs to be a strong support system for them when they do so. The following section highlights this issue.

A Support System

A strong support system while they were recovering was paramount for several of the men. Participants talked about the importance of the support they received from counselors and friends they met while attending such meetings in AA and/or NA. They also highlighted the importance of ongoing support from family members. Nick talked about the support he received from family as a key factor in his recovery:

> I would say for me it was like I say there was a lot of support, positive support … you got kids that love you. A lot of prayer and support of loved ones and friends you know, kind of took the place to where I said to myself, you know, "I don't need it in my life," 'cause at one time I thought I did need it.

Trent explained that he received a lot of support from a mentor who he met in a recovery program as he stated: "It kinda has to be somebody you just meet and you just realize me and this person click really well and they've been through this stuff and they're better now." Trent also talked about the role his family played in his recovery: "A big part of mine was family. I've seen a few people that didn't recover because they didn't have family behind 'em or helping to pick them back up." D also noted the importance of having a mentor who had also suffered through addiction and entered recovery:

> It's really instrumental to sobriety, to know that there's somebody who's been through what you've been through, and they've been able to pull out of it and they're happier, you know, 'cause at the time I wouldn't thought I could be any happier, you know, what else did I have to look forward to? What did I have to live for? You know, the next fix was all I really had. It was work and drugs, work and drugs, and I didn't have anything else really in my life.

Aaron also felt that it is important for men to be able to talk to other men who have been through the process. For Aaron, an important factor in his recovery "was a guy talking to a guy, which guys can feel and understand each other." David felt that

> You definitely need to have some kind of support if you're going into the rehab. You definitely have to have some support when you get out.

Duane's comments were insightful as he stated that one has to be in the very middle of their recovery:

I think you've got to put yourself in the middle of it, um, yesterday, I talked to my sponsor, and I talked to both the guys I sponsor, see how I'm in the middle there, I got my hand in my sponsor's hand, I got my hand in these people's hand and, um, and I get to be a part of it that way and I, and it's first, it's absolutely first , it comes before school, it comes before work, it comes before relationships, it comes before family, uh, my relationship with God and Alcoholics Anonymous are absolutely the most important thing.

Bishop clarified his views:

You've got to reach a point in your life where you say, you know, I want something different and you have to really mean it, I'd guess you'd call it surrendering. And you can't do it alone, that's how a lot of them go wrong, they try to do it alone. I found that the best way to sustain my recovery was to stay involved with a fellowship of peers like people who have lived the life that I have lived. They have learned how to stay clean so for me recovery when I see it, it is a complete lifestyle change. It meant that I had to change my way of thinking about life in general. You do it one day at a time. You do it by staying positive, staying focused on goals, being consistent, ah, and incorporating spiritual forces within your life. That's what works for me.

Other factors were also highlighted among participants. Most of the men noted that these factors may vary amongst individuals. Some participants stressed the fact that, first, one must be ready to change and must want to go into recovery. Second, some men stressed the importance of the need to address circumstances that may influence substance use. And, finally, several men also noted that support was vital in one's recovery.

Recovery as a Lifelong Process

When thinking about their definition of recovery, six men described it as an ongoing, lifelong process meaning that there is the need to change their lives completely. Several men also explained that recovery is not simply abstaining from using particular substances, but also changing one's entire lifestyle and finally gaining control over their lives. For example, Travis stated that:

My definition of recovery is it is a lifelong process because I will never be recovered from anything, you know. It's just like learning how to do a trade in my opinion because you're always learning something new to better yourself.

Nick explained that in order to get to recovery one has to "let go, you know, when you're ready." Nick also described recovery as a one day process each and every day:

> A one day process, ah, each and every day, you know, you get things, and I do believe in a higher power who I call Jesus Christ. I know that giving him a chance within my life – because I've done all the wrongs, so I am going to do what's right. You know, and truthfully, to tell you the truth, I don't know how I did it today. I just don't mess with it.

D also sees recovery as "a lifelong process. It's never gone, I mean, you have a problem, and that problem's gonna stay with you."

Other participants also noted that recovery means a total change of their lives and as Bishop reiterated: "It's not, just not using drugs, it's changing their lifestyle." When asked if recovery was a process that one took one day at a time, Kid answered that: "Sometimes it's an hour, or five minutes or even a minute at a time."

Some participants defined recovery as becoming aware of the impact their addiction was having on their own lives and on others around them. JT described it as an awakening, where "something clicked in my mind and said that is stupid, what am I doing?" When defining recovery, Buck saw it as "becoming aware of the consequences of your actions and the effects on others."

When asked about recovery, Oreste explained:

> I began to recognize what it was doing to my life. I couldn't do that and be the father I needed to be. Recovery is the recognition of exactly how bad your addiction is, the pain it is bringing to others and recognizing what you have to do in order to eliminate the act of addiction in your life.

Duane defined it as finally having the ability to "see the truth" and being "able to breathe." Daved noted that recovery was a "period of growth." For Aaron, recovery meant "coming face to face with your demons and letting go of all the hurt, pain that accompanied it and finally facing the truth about yourself, and that you're not going to use anymore."

Herb also reiterated how his previous actions had hurt those close to him:

> Now, my conscious has changed, I actually have one now, so, I realized my actions don't only affect me, it affects a whole lot of people around me. If I was to use, it wouldn't only affect me, but my

children, my brothers and my father, they all got the trust back, you know, the love and everything, it would affect a whole lot of people, you know, and the men around me who look up to me in recovery. I have to realize my actions every day, see life is a whole bunch of choices and you have a choice every day, whether you're going to use or not.

Oliver defined recovery as:

Not being active in what you were addicted to, without that nemesis, that monkey on your back constantly; it's like you're freed from a, from the monkey, we – I always refer to it, you've heard that term, monkey on the back, it, it, to me, it's a conscious freedom of, of that monkey.

Timex explained that recovery is the ability to get away from the addiction and to finally control it. For another participant, Sterling, recovery is "when you no longer have that need." Similarly, for Martin recovery meant "breaking that dependence. Finding something that gives you the strength or just the discipline to break that and form new habits that are better." He continued to elaborate:

It's so many things; mostly for me it's the ability to see the truth, to see that stuff I felt whenever I was a child just wasn't true and just because I feel it, doesn't make it a fact and, um, to be able to see the difference between that and not have to act upon however it is I'm feeling and, um, and so basically, recovery does the same thing for me that alcohol and drugs do and it makes me able to breathe.

Perhaps D stated it the best when he expanded on how he felt as he processed his recovery:

I know, but I believe there's a foundation that you're built upon and it's your choice, you can raise it to the ground and build it back up the way you want to, it's just a foundation, it doesn't mean that's what the building has to be like. And I think your life's kinda like that too, I mean it kinda supports, you know, I mean, just because you're raised prejudice doesn't mean you're gonna grow up to be prejudice, that's something that you can change, and I think, you know, violence and stuff that happens in your past is the same way, you don't have to keep it inside, you don't have to hold onto it and let it eat you.

For Rock, his recovery meant a total change of his life:

Recovery to me means a whole total change of life. It's not just being abstinent from drugs, it's a change of my entire life from the things I used to believe in, from the things I used to do, that today I won't do. Because for one thing my heart has been changed and I don't want to repeat the lifestyle that I lived. So, my recovery is an ongoing process, you know, and it's a one day at a time journey.

Kid related his recovery to having a problem:

It starts with admitting that you have a problem, or that you cannot control something, you know … recovery … recovery is, recovery is actually beating whatever you got the problem with. If you're in recovery, you're beating it at that time.

Bobo stated that for him, recovery was: "almost like doin' everything the opposite of what I been doin' and I think it's just bein' a responsible person, somethin' that we never was." For Oreste recovery is relatable to the pain it brings to others in one's life. And for Martin, recovery is breaking his dependence and "finding something that gives you the strength or just the discipline to break that and form new habits that are better."

When asked their definition of recovery, participants offered thoughtful and insightful views that involved not only changing one's entire lifestyle and finally gaining control over their lives but also having a philosophy about living that now "fit" within their lives.

In the literature there is no mention of how men (or women for that matter) feel about the other sex in their use of drugs and/or alcohol. I decided in my interviews that this would be an interesting question to ask and I was rewarded with insightful answers as to these men's attitudes towards women's use of drugs and/or alcohol as highlighted in the following discussion.

Men and Women: Differences in Addiction and Recovery

The literature shows that when it comes to terminating substance misuse, women are presented with very unique challenges compared to their male counterparts. Severe substance misuse holds substantially different physiological as well as social implications for women than for men; the physiological effects of regular substance misuse, particularly alcohol, on women can be much more destructive for them than for men; the social taboos against women having problems with alcohol and other forms of drugs produce more shame and guilt for them than for their male counterparts and can create barriers for seeking help; and substance use can be a form of temporary escape from the negative affective states associated with higher rates of mental health problems experienced by women who use drugs (Cloud and Granfield 2008). As seen by their answers documented below, my participants seemingly understood the various factors that impact on women's use/abuse of substances.

David felt that men and women are similar in their recovery and thought that in some areas there may be better programs in place to help female users. Kid also felt that there were appropriate resources for women. He explained that in terms of "mentality" men and women were similar. Rock also felt that men and women were similar when it comes to recovery:

> I don't think there's really any difference if a person really got his mind, heart made up, if a person really wants to change, really wants to do something different. I don't think it makes a difference if it's male or female.

Bishop also explained his ideas:

> As far as having the will power, I don't think there's any difference than a woman or a man because our program teaches us an addict any addict, it says an addict can lose the desire to use, can stop using and find a new way of life.

Nick also stated his opinions in terms of women's addiction: "I think it's harder on a woman 'cause it seems like it does something to them more than it does to a man … it tears them down quicker than it does the man."

For Daved, his comments were thorough:

> You know, it seems like I've read about something like that, I don't know what the numbers show but I think there is a difference, and that's because, you know, the thing with women, and I've read many women's stories about alcoholism and recovery and so forth and so on, and, uh, I think the difference is because they are women, it's that prejudice or that that old stigmatism or whatever, you know.

He also noted that there is a difference among women who have entered recovery. He went on to describe an experience he had while attending a meeting for recovering addicts:

> This girl came through, and everybody had a crush on her, and she ended up having to leave because all she was doing was getting hit on by the guys in there.

There were several participants who discussed the sexual and physical abuse of women related to their addiction. For Bishop, he noted the difficulties facing female addicts:

> It is much harder for a woman to be an addict, because women are vulnerable, men can take advantage of women a lot easier. Women have something to offer and they can really, really get abused. I do believe that women have more issues coming into recovery than men do.

Many of the participants explained that women are vulnerable to men who will use them for sex. For example, D spoke bluntly when he stated:

> I'd never been raped, you know, I've never had to go through that because I've been messed up on drugs. I've never got the shit kicked out of me by somebody where I couldn't defend myself ... there's the difference, and, as an addict, I think that you have more respect when you walk in, and you're a man, than you tend to as you're a woman.

Several of the other participants also talked about the fact that women prostitute themselves in order to support their habit. Many of the men were very aware of the profound effects of prostitution on female addicts. D explained further: "Because I've seen that to where it – women just go all out, you know, on the street, on the corner." Bobo also felt that "it's harder for them to recover than it is men ... they throw away a lot more." When asked what they threw away, Bobo said that "their body and I actually think when they get deep into that; it's harder for them to come out of it."

When asked if he felt it was harder for a woman to recover, Buck responded:

> It is. It's a lot harder. There's so much that a woman's gotta do, that she's gonna regret, and the abuse that happens to them, and it's a lot harder for a woman to recover from being an addict, that I've seen, and a lot of the times they don't.

Buck also explained how physical and sexual abuse can greatly affect a women's self-worth. Harvey noted that when it comes to addiction and recovery "it screws women up a lot more than men."

Oliver also discussed the issues female addicts must face and the damaging effects of prostitution:

I see a lot of addicted women, but I, I, it's gotta be pretty difficult for 'em. I think from what I've seen, a lot of women are dependent on men for their addiction. They use together, but a lot of times they have to do things for their drugs. I mean I never had to trade my body for anything that I wanted, you know, uh, I know a lot of women that have to, and I, I think that would have to be awful, awful hard. I think even when they try to look at their self in the mirror, they realize that they're something to use, they don't really have an identity, they're something, they're a usable item.

Several men discussed the challenge that female addicts are faced with when they have children. Oliver explained that often when there are children involved, the man will leave and the mother is left to take care of them, all the while suffering from an addiction.

Sherman also expressed his views on women with children:

From what I've seen in these three years I would hate to be a woman in recovery. I've seen, they have problems as far as dealing with, trying to get kids back and stuff like that; it's much rougher for a woman. Just there's more pressure. Women have always had to carry a family and then today where a lot of women don't have a male figure to help carry them, you understand what I'm saying?

He went on to reiterate: "With my kid's moms and stuff like that … I tell them thank you all the time for being a mother and a father because, 'cause it's like real rough." Aaron also talked about his adopted sister and noted that it was particularly difficult for her to enter recovery because she had children. He explained the guilt she felt in leaving her children.

A few participants also noted that there is more of a stigma associated with female drug addicts. For example, Daved felt that there is a difference among men and women because of society's belief that women are not "supposed" to do drugs. He agreed that women who use are judged more harshly than men. Oreste stated that when it comes to women,

The addiction perhaps has a social stigma, that is, men are thought of as the drunk who will never get over it, and women are seen as the horrible mother who's abandoning her children, so there's a different view, the stigmas different. Because the standards seem higher because they're mothers.

Oreste expanded on his views:

Um, so I think it's, I think ultimately, sociologically, um, the judgment is harsher on women than men. I think that the, the addiction is understood more for a man than it is for a woman. I think it's considered more a male, a male problem than it is a female problem and the woman is not only failing herself and her parents but more important her children. Nobody bothers indicting a man; they don't indict a man as much … over the horrible things … kids on the same level, so I think it's worse for women sociologically. I think that, I think addiction itself is an omnivorous beast that doesn't care if you're male or female.

Travis suggested that women are more worried about what other people will think about them as he stated: "You know, if they find out they're drunks or something like that, you know, than the whole town is going to know."

Nick stated that in his view:

Because the thing is, the things that they go through, they had to go through trying to recover because – not so much our surroundings, but I believe the woman, you know, they got what it takes to get some, you know, really, they don't, you know, they sell their body, you know, stuff like, like, they can prostitute themselves. Like I'm saying that's what some of them like, sex and the trade, you know what I'm saying, cause I've seen that before but, ah, yeah, I think it's harder on a woman cause it seems like it does something to them more than it does to a man. On the woman, she, it tears them down quicker than it does the man. Because I've seen that to where it – women just go all out, you know, on the street, on the corner, sleep right here, do this, do that, you know, ah, five guys, two guys, you know what I'm saying. I know some girls that they like that.

Leonard was certainly honest in his approach:

Guys, they … most of these guys that are really hittin' it hard drug use like me, you know, by the time they get to their 30s early 40s, they start, I mean they got no game left man, they're just crashing and burning and hittin' too hard, and it seems like, now of course statistics would bear it out … but it seems like women tend to get by, of course, this isn't sexist on my part, but boy once a woman has hit a certain point, no one wants fuckin' shit to do with her man, and she is really cut off high and dry.

Harvey also suggested that in his view:

It screws women up a lot more than men. It just whoops them out real bad, especially speed, speed, speed will destroy a woman.

Several of the men noted that there were specific differences among female and male addicts. They felt that these differences make it harder for women to enter recovery. Although men also face several challenges and must also deal with many issues in their addiction and recovery, female addicts face different challenges simply because they are women. Women must also deal with physical and sexual abuse. Many female addicts are vulnerable to some men who are eager to manipulate them because of their addiction and use them for sex. Often, women prostitute themselves for drugs which can have a profound effect on their self-worth. Participants also noted that some women have to deal with the challenge of having children while suffering from an addiction. Women must also deal with the added stigma associated with female drug addicts. And some participants noted that there may also be a lack of resources that target women's needs in particular areas.

Overall, these participants were very aware of both subtle and major differences between their use/abuse of substances and women's, offering their views that in most if not all circumstances, it is much harder for a woman to leave her addiction.

Suggestions for Change

Although many suggestions for change for all individuals formerly addicted to substances can be made, a few of the men were very vocal about their ideas of what was important for their lives and those of others as the following comments show. For example, D talked about drug courts and highlighted their importance in helping those suffering from addiction:

> It's an age-old question ... you know, does it work, doesn't it work? That's the same thing with drug addiction. You don't know it's gonna work until it grabs you. I've had my first die in my arms, I've been shot, I've almost OD'd. I've watched my friends OD and none of that made me stop, you know.

D continued:

> I think drug courts are incredible! Because they give people the education, and the ability to know, and like I said, they may not use it then, they may use it a couple years down the road, but I mean, if you look at the recidivism rates and the self-reports on their usage of drugs, people that go through drug courts have a way higher percentage chance of not doing drugs and they have a lower recidivism rate than people, than of nonparticipants. I think we need to get people on the

same page, like the counselors on the same page. I think we need to get on the same page as far as what drug addiction is. Maybe you shouldn't treat people that have crimes against others that are drug addicts, you know, maybe you should let them go to prison, but make sure that there's treatment available to them in prison.

Within less than a decade, virtually every state in the United States has implemented a drug court. Drug courts utilize numerous strategies for processing, controlling, and treating drug use. The primary mission of the drug court is to stop or reduce drug and alcohol use and related criminal activity. In addition, the drug court model is designed to decrease case-processing time, alleviate the demand of drug-related cases on the court system, reduce jail and prison commitments, increase offender accountability, and provide a more cost-effective means of controlling drug offenders compared to incarceration (Johnson et al. 2003).

Bishop also discussed the importance of the elements of recovery:

I think one of the single most factors in my recovery that happened to get me this far is that when I went to the prison treatment program that I work at now, I began to identify with a new belief system and I began to understand that I need a structure in my life. A lot of people rebel against structure because all that is, is me wanting to be in control and I know I don't have to be in control today, you know, if I can lead a structured life by doing the simple things that normal people get up and do every day then most of all the things I'm confronted with have a happy ending, so that's it.

Leonard stated that he is a strong believer in 90-day treatment programs and explained that government support and programs can play a key role in helping others enter recovery: "As far as long-term recovery goes, I know a lot of guys that got clean by the government footing the bill and helping them." Leonard went on to explain that chances of success are higher when one has the opportunity to simply focus on recovery.

Other participants gave a few last words of advice. Timex noted that he cannot tell others not to drink, however, he can tell them to drink responsibly. He also stated:

If you plan on drivin' [while drinking] have somebody else … somebody else drive. My dad taught me right off the bat; he said that is the quickest way to lose your life.

Kid stated:

> The only thing ... that I would like to add is, I hope that anything I might have said today ... can help someone out there in their addiction, whether it be drinking, shootin', poppin' snortin' whatever their addiction is ... whatever, an addiction is an addiction, and ... until, if you can beat it, beat it. Whatever it takes ... actually the best thing I can tell someone is ... you have to ... to beat an addiction, you have to say no, you have to want to say no, more than you have to want to say yes.

Two participants talked about the impact of certain societal factors on substance use such as the responsibility of society as a whole to help those suffering from addiction. Bishop stated:

> I think society as a whole needs to view addiction with a broad understanding that many, many people are in addiction ... cultural issues, urban issues, depending on where you live, those things come into play. But once a person becomes addicted, once a person is addicted, society has an obligation to understand what addiction is and understand that anybody is capable of becoming an addict. It gets back to choices. People choose to use, but those that are deeply in addiction, they don't have a choice; they lost their choice to walk away. Just walk away – you *can't* – just walk away [Bishop's emphasis].

Sherman noted his concern for the lack of programs available to addicts in smaller communities. Sherman is able to attend a meeting every day of the week, yet he pointed out that in smaller communities, one may be lucky to attend a meeting once or twice a week. He went on to voice his concern over the war on drugs in the United States:

> Sending someone to jail for over a year and what is that gonna do? Nothing. That's just going to make that person more bitter and there's probably more dope inside of a prison than there is out here on the streets. 'Cause you send someone to prison, that doesn't ... stop the cycle. Prison ain't gonna do nothing, it's just gonna harden me up.

Another participant, Oliver, stated with optimism that:

> I never dreamed that I would ever have any happiness in my life and I know that without, without the addiction in my life, I'm, I realize happiness, you know, it doesn't take, you know, big cars, big money, big fancy suit to ... be happy, happy is, uh, a state of mind, you know. My mind works well enough now to allow me to be happy and feel, to

feel emotions that I've never felt before ... I, don't have the feelings of, of you know, no self-esteem. The way I was raised and what I went through all my life, uh, I feel like I'm, I'm good, you know. I have everything in the world to be thankful for, you know, and nothing to be ashamed of, and nothing to hide my head about.

For Martin having a mentor was of paramount importance:

I think, to be successful at any point in life, you need a mentor especially in recovery, cuz that's, that's nothing you want to go through alone even though a little bit of, I call it a little bit of recovery cuz I didn't go to a program or whatever but I, I did have that, that guy there with me, my youth pastor and now my best friend, uh, not the same guy but, we went through it together, you know, he didn't understand, you know, my best friend didn't understand where I was coming from, he had never done that, um, he didn't really understand the mental state I was in or whatever, but he was there, and he listened and he was strength for me when I was, when I was being a little weak, you know.

Duane's suggestion was insightful:

The only thing that we have is our experience. Um, and guys like me could go in and share our experiences and those people that are on the borderline but were not gonna try it, you might be able to sway in one way or another. I think the very best thing we should do is, just educate 'em and let them know, if they ever get tired [of] that way of life, there is a solution for 'em.

For Herb, his advice was wise and practical:

I try to tell these young guys, not as in age, but as in recovery, you gotta work the steps man, it's the most incredible thing you'll ever do, and actually the steps work for a whole lot of different things, not just addiction, you know. If you don't have the desire to stop doing something, you're not gonna do it. People can talk to you all day, give you books, you can read it, you can have all the information on the planet about something but if you don't have the desire within you to stop doing something, you're not gonna stop doing something, it's just not gonna happen, you're just wasting your time and other people's time.

When thinking about ways in which we, as a society, can better help those suffering from addiction, it is important to take their concerns and suggestions into consideration. They have lived through addiction and who better can understand what factors must be in place to help others recover? Implementing policies which take such concerns into consideration could be successful in helping more addicts enter recovery. The following section highlights such policies as well as suggestions for further work in the area of men's addiction and recovery experiences.

Suggestions for Policy Initiatives

Participants have narrated their experiences of addiction and recovery throughout this book offering the reader some understanding of their lives. Taking a lead from the men's voices, I offer in this section some policy initiatives in order to assist individuals in their challenges as they struggle to recover from their addiction to substances. First, however, I highlight a bit of a background from various authors about their views of the drug problem, both in the United States and other countries around the world.

In society today, drug and alcohol abuse constitute a significant and worrying health problem that will not go away without some substantive changes to this problem. Drugs have overall "been construed as health or societal dangers by modern states, medical authorities, and regulatory cultures and are now globally prohibited in production, use, and sale" (Gootenberg 2009, p. 1). Gootenberg (2009, p. 14) further states that "the global trade in illicit drugs—worth about $300 to $500 billion in "street sales" annually—is among the world's largest commodity trades, everywhere in tandem with other flows and institutions, despite massive efforts at control." Hallam and Bewley-Taylor (2010, p. 3) argue that

> The complexities of the contemporary world demand a new mapping, sensitive to the facts of human suffering, the collateral damage of forms of drug control and the realities of social change.

Furthermore, Goode (1999) stresses most succinctly that we should "quit dreaming of a drug-free America, because that is a literal impossibility" (p. 418).

As a response to the problem of drug abuse, national drug policies have emphasized punishment over treatment, and in a manner that has had a disproportionate impact on low-income minority communities. After millions of people are arrested and incarcerated, it is clear that the "war on drugs" has reshaped the way America responds to crime and ushered in an era of instability and mistrust in countless communities (Mauer and King 2007).

Mauer and King (2007) further argue that by the mid-1990s, the climate regarding drug policy in the United States had shifted somewhat, reflecting a growing frustration with the "lock 'em up" strategy to addressing drug abuse and growing support for the treatment model of combating drug abuse. The result was the proliferation of drug courts and other alternative sentencing strategies that sought to divert low-level drug offenders from prison into community-based treatment programs. Despite the expansion of these options over the last decade, the punitive sentencing provisions of the 1980s remain in effect across the United States, resulting in a record number of arrests, convictions, and sentences to prison for drug offenses.

However, not all nations follow the American model; Europe is a good working example of the revised approach to drug policy in which the user is treated as a responsible citizen. A major part of the European model of drug policy is to treat drug use not as a criminal activity, but rather a part of human nature that should best be handled in a manner that minimizes adverse effects to both the individual and society as a whole. European countries largely believe that the way to approach drug use is to emphasize truthful education over propaganda and promotion of self-development over repressive law enforcement. Most of Europe has recognized that the criminal justice system only exacerbates problems associated with drug use by causing social stigma and an increased sense of failure and self-esteem for the user. Instead, a more pro-active and holistic approach is utilized in deterring drug use instead of a reactionary one (Gatto 2002; Grant 2009).

Correspondingly, Degenhardt, Hallam and Bewley-Taylor (2009) argue that the Netherlands and Sweden are usually signified as representing different poles in terms of their drug policies, with the Dutch having a pragmatic, liberal approach and Sweden's restrictive policies being grounded in their vision of a drug-free society. Similarly, Portugal has adopted some singular legal measures in recent years, and Germany has been particularly innovative in its treatment and public health policies.

Most European countries firmly believe that there can be no legal basis for prohibiting freedom of action in respect to one's own body. This "European" mentality of freedom to conduct one's personal affairs while respecting the rights of others stands as an example to the United States and other countries. Gatto (2002) argues that when a tolerant and compassionate view toward drug use and drug users is realized, inevitably, nations begin to see a noticeable improvement in the quality of life for its citizens.

As well, in Canada, most drug policy is based mainly on the harm reduction model, a policy or program directed towards decreasing the adverse health, social, and economic consequences of drug abuse without requiring abstinence from such use (MacPherson 2001). This approach responds to those who need treatment for addiction, while clearly stressing that public disorder, including the open drug scene, must be stopped. Harm reductionists contend that no one should be denied services, such as health care and Social Security, merely because they take certain risks or exhibit certain behaviors that are generally disapproved of by society as a whole, or its laws. Further, harm reduction seeks to take a social justice stance in response to behaviors such as the use of illicit drugs, as opposed to criminalizing and prosecuting these behaviors. Often, harm reduction advocates view the prohibition of drugs discriminatory, ineffective and counter-productive. Among other arguments, they point out that the burden placed on the public health system and society as a whole from cannabis use and other illegal drugs are relatively low (Grant 2009; MacPherson 2001).

Riley (1998) suggests that persisting in current drug policies will only result in more drug use, more empowerment of drug markets and criminals, and more disease and suffering. He argues that drug laws must be reexamined and alternative means of reducing the harms associated with drugs in society must be honestly and openly considered. Drugs should be treated as a health, social, and political issue rather than a criminal one (Riley 1998).

So, in offering the above discussion on drug use/abuse, a significant question to be asked is, "Where do we go from here?"

First, there is an overall need to validate men's suggestions (and women's as well for that matter) for what works in the field of addiction and recovery; we need to listen to what individuals who are former drug addicts have to say. As Stevens et al. (2007) argue we need to amplify the voices of the people who experience these problems and enable them to explain their own choices and needs. It is key that people in recovery lead the way; in other words, people must take ownership of his or her own recovery process. Zuber-Skerritt (2001, p. 15) states, "We come to know and learn from our action/experience, but whatever we have conceptualized and learnt must lead to action, improvement, development or change." Having worked in the field for so many years, I argue that individuals who are former addicts have a lot to offer as their experiences have enabled them to become "experts" in the fields of addiction and recovery.

Second, as D suggested earlier, drug courts work and much of the evaluation of such courts show that they do as well. The drug court model is based on the premise that a more flexible approach to treating drug-addicted offenders, in combination with increased court involvement and oversight of offender's treatment progress, will result in less drug dependency and lower rates of recidivism (Johnson et al. 2003, p. 406).

Third, make sure that all individuals who work in the field (i.e., counselors) are "on the same page" (D) as far as what drug addiction is. Individuals who counsel addicts within the system need to understand the following: there must be active involvement by the individuals impacted by drug use/abuse including daily decision-making that is necessary for initiating and sustaining recovery; this means that recovery is enhanced by a person-environment fit. This includes involvement from policy development through service delivery and evaluation.

We need to understand that there are multiple pathways and styles of recovery as many of the participants in this study have highlighted. Participants also talked about how their recovery flourished in their supportive communities (i.e., family, friends, work and school). As many participants in this study also suggested, recovery is not only voluntary but also a longitudinal and developmental process that includes peers and significant others to help them on their journeys. As Martin stated:

> I think, to be successful at any point in life, you need a mentor especially in recovery, cuz that's, that's nothing you want to go through alone.

Fourth, enable addicts within the prison system to access the treatment available. For Bishop, one of the single most important factors in his recovery was the prison program that he was able to access. In his treatment program, he "began to identify with a new belief system," meaning that he began to understand that he needed structure in his life, something that was somewhat new to him. Further, Bishop stated it very well when he said,

> I think society as a whole needs to view addiction with a broad understanding that many, many people are in addiction … cultural issues, urban issues, depending on where you live, those things come into play.

Here I further contend that any understanding of how to deal with the drug problem must be framed within the confines of poverty, unemployment, economic security, and access to education and proper health care. Gordon (1994) also states that while drug prevention and treatment have traditionally focused on changing individual behaviors, such efforts can have only limited impact when changes are not made to the environment, that is, to the social determinants of drug use. These include the social and cultural environment, the economic environment, and the physical environment (Gordon 1994).

Currie (1987, Abstract) further argues that reduced legitimate economic opportunities will increase the attractiveness of illicit drug trafficking, and current criminal justice policies which overemphasize the use of overcrowded and brutalizing prisons will increase rather than decrease criminality. Both "street" and business crimes are likely to increase under current trends. Public policy should halt the growing split between the rich and poor, provide early education for disadvantaged children, supply family economic and social supports, and encourage crime prevention programs. Young (n.d.) further states that

> We oppose reforms whether punitive or medical which serve to capture the drug user in his or her role and social predicament and we support those which genuinely change the social predicament and de-essentialise drug use. (n.p.)

From my work in the field, I also offer the following views and suggestions regarding drug use/abuse. Recently, the *Drug Report*, published by the United Nations in 2008 advocates for the following issues to be at the forefront of any drug policies worldwide thus adding to the foregoing critical arguments (Costa 2008). Public health – the first principle of drug control – should be brought back to center stage. Currently, the amount of resources and political support for public security and law enforcement far outweigh those devoted to public health. This must be rebalanced. Drug dependence is an illness that should be treated like any other. More resources are needed to prevent people from taking drugs, to treat those who are dependent, and to reduce the adverse health and social consequences of drug abuse (Costa 2008, p. 1).

Protecting public security and safeguarding public health should be done in a way that upholds human rights and human dignity. For example, nonmedical use of psychoactive drugs is inevitable in any society that has access to such drugs. Drug policies cannot be based on a utopian belief that nonmedical drug use will be eliminated. Drug policies cannot be based on a utopian belief that all drug users will always use drugs safely. Further, drug policies must be pragmatic. They must be assessed on their actual consequences, not on whether they symbolically send the right, the wrong or mixed messages (Davidson, Tondora and O'Connell 2007).

Drug users are an integral part of the larger community. Protecting the health of the community as a whole therefore requires protecting the health of drug users, and this requires integrating the drug users within the community rather than attempting to isolate them from it. Drug use leads to individual and social harms through many different mechanisms, so a wide range of interventions is needed to address these harms. These interventions include providing health care (including drug abuse treatment) to current drug users; reducing the numbers of persons who are likely to begin using some drugs; and, particularly, enabling users to switch to safer forms of drug use. It is not always necessary to reduce nonmedical drug use in order to reduce harms (Davidson et al. 2007).

Further, as Sussman et al. (2008) argue, it is essential, ideally, that the treatment intervention, along with treatment setting and services, should be matched to the particular problems and needs of the individual (engaging and developing their strengths and minimizing the influences of their limitations), given the realities of available resources, while promoting viable reduction of harm and facilitating a quality of life in which well-being and satisfaction are indices of recovery.

In conclusion, I offer the argument that the participants in this study found real alternatives by which they could guide their lives and continue in a new direction as they processed recovery. I have gained much needed knowledge as I interviewed the men and documented their narratives of their addiction and recovery processes. They have reevaluated their lives in an important way and my hope is that they continue to have the courage to continue on their pathways to recovery.

Appendix

Questionnaire

A. History of Drug Use/Abuse:

First of all, I would like to ask you a few questions about your substance abuse.

At what age did you first start to use controlled substances? Where did you start to use?

What did you first use when addicted? Did you use a lot of drugs? If so, what were they?

Are there any members of your immediate or extended family (mother, father, siblings, grandparents, cousins, etc.) that used controlled substances? If so, what did they use and for how long?

Tell me your definition of addiction, of recovery.

How did you first start to use? What got you started? Why did you start? What was going on in your life at that time - any specific events/conditions occurring?

How long were you addicted?

How much did you use? What was the extent of your drug use - I mean by that, how much did you use say, per day/per week? A lot, a little, moderate use?

What was your primary or favorite drug that you used overall? Why was that your favorite drug? What did drugs "do" for you?

Describe for me how you were feeling or thinking at that time. Describe for me how drugs made you feel when you were using. Describe for me how you saw yourself when you were addicted.

How does one get addicted? How did you get addicted? Can you tell me your ideas about that?

Did anyone influence your using/abusing controlled substances?

Did you make any major adjustments in your life at the time of your using drugs?

Describe for me any impact on your family life (immediate family/children/partners) at the time of your addiction? What was your relationship like with your family, children, partners, and nonusing friends at the time?

Were your friendship networks changing? If so, tell me about that.

Who were your friends/community at that time? Did they influence you in any way? If so, how?

Did you work/school/study while addicted? Describe for me what it was like while working, going to school and/or studying while using?

B. History of Recovery:

Let's look now at how you first thought about going into recovery.

What was going on in your life when you began to think about recovery? How did you make the decision to quit? Tell me a bit about how you were thinking and feeling at that time.

When did all this come about? Where? How long ago? How old were you when you quit?

How long have you been abstinent?

Were there specific events or conditions at that time that began to influence your decision to stop using controlled substances?

How did you make the final choice to quit?

Did anyone influence/try to influence you at this time? Tell me about that.

Did you go for outside help, i.e., AA or NA or therapy of any kind, when you first decided to get off drugs? Tell me about that.

Did you have to make any major adjustments in your life when you decided to stop using? Describe that for me.

Did you have or do anything different in your life at this time? (Probe for examples such as new work, new interests, hobbies, friends, new partner).

What took the place of drugs in your life when you went into recovery?

How did you tell others in your life (your family, using friends) that you were no longer using controlled substances? How did they react to your decision? Tell me about that.

Were your friendship networks changing, that is, with user friends, nonusers, old partners, new partners in your life? If so, tell me about that.

How were you feeling or thinking at that time? (Probe for feelings of relief, feeling anxious, feeling lost, isolated, rootless, or afraid of the unknown, a "vacuum" experience, tension, stress, for feelings of being in control, being fearful, inner conflicts, sense of autonomy, feeling free, confident, empowered, stable in life).

What factors need to be in place for men to go into recovery?

What was the "key" to your recovery?

What do you think it takes to be successful in recovery? Why, do you think, you were finally successful in giving up your abuse of drugs?

Have other people helped you to maintain your decision not to use controlled substances? If so, who are they and how important are they to you?

How do you feel about controlled substances now?

What was the most significant thing that you can think of that helped you to recover from your addiction?

What has been the most difficult thing(s) you had to deal with in your recovery?

Describe for me what your recovery has been like generally.

We know from studies on addiction/recovery that people practice giving up their addiction; in other words, they don't go in a straight line to recovery. Has that been your experience? So, how did you do it?

Do you view your recovery in specific phases or stages? If so, describe that for me

How did you deal with society's reactions to you at that time; in other words, were people treating you differently now that you were in recovery? Describe that for me.

Do you think that being a man made it harder or easier to leave your addiction? Do you think it is different from how a woman is treated?

Describe for me your new lifestyle. How does it differ from your old lifestyle?

Do you feel you gained a new identity for yourself since leaving the use of drugs? If so, describe that for me.

Describe for me your "old self" and now your "new self." Do you think you have a new "self" now? Do you see yourself differently now? If so, how do you see yourself differently?

Have you taken any steps backward in your recovery in the past? In other words, did you ever relapse? How did you deal with that?

Do you take steps backward in your recovery now? If so, how do you deal with them?

Did this period of your life (recovery) take a short or long period of time? Tell me about that.

What do you consider your greatest achievement up to this point in your life?

Do you have plans for the near and far future? If so, describe them for me.

Thank you for your time. Is there anything else you would like to add before we finish?

Bibliography

Abbot, A. A. 1995. Substance use and the feminist perspective. In *Feminist practice in the 21st century,* edited by N. Van Den Bergh, 258–78. Washington, DC: National Association of Social Workers Press.

Adrian, M., C. Lundy, and M. Eliany, (eds.). 1996. *Canadian women and substance use: Overview and policy implications.* Toronto, Ontario: Addiction Research Foundation.

Anderson, T. 1991. Identity transformation in drug addiction. Unpublished doctoral dissertation, American University, Washington, DC.

Anderson, T., and L. Bondi. 1998. Exiting the drug-addict role: Variations by race and gender. *Symbolic Interaction, 21*(2), 155–174.

Baer, D. J., and J. J. Corrado. 1974. Heroin addict relationships with parents during childhood and early adolescent years. *The Journal of Genetic Psychology, 124*(1), 99–103.

Bacon, S. D. 1973. The process of addiction to alcohol. Social aspects. *Quarterly Journal of Studies on Alcohol,34*(1), 1–27.

Bahr, S. J., A. C. Marcos, and S. L. Maughan. 1995. Family, educational and peer influences on the alcohol use of female and male adolescents. *Journal of Studies on Alcohol, 56,* 457–469.

Bateson, G. (1972). *Steps to an ecology of mind.* New Jersey: Northvale.

Bean, M. (1975). Alcoholics Anonymous: II. *Psychiatric Annals, 5*(3), 83–117.

Becker, H. 1953. Becoming a marijuana user. *American Journal of Sociology, 59,* 235–42.

Becker, H. 1960. Notes on the concept of commitment. *American Journal of Sociology, 66,* 32–42.

Benoliel, J. Q. 2001. Expanding knowledge about women through grounded theory: Introduction to the collection. *Health Care for Women International, 22,* 7–9.

Beverley, J. 2000. "Testimonio, Subalternity, and Narrative Authority," in N. K. Denzin and Y. S. Lincoln (eds) *Handbook of qualitative research,* 2nd Edition, pp. 555–565. Thousand Oaks, CA: Sage.

Biernacki, P. 1986. *Pathways from heroin addiction: Recovery without treatment.* Philadelphia: Temple University Press.

Bierut, L. J., J. R. Strickland, J. R., Thompson, S. E. Afful, and L. B. Cottler. 2008. Drug use and dependence in cocaine dependent subjects, community based individuals and their siblings. *Drug and Alcohol Dependence, 95,* 14–22.

Blackwell, J., W. E. Thurston, and K. Graham. 1996. Women's use of alcohol, tobacco and other drugs in Canada. In *Canadian women and substance use: Overview and policy implications,* edited by M. Adrian, C. Lundy, and M. Eliany, 228–46. Toronto, Ontario: Addiction Research Foundation.

Blood, L., and A. Cornwall. 1996. Childhood sexual victimization as a factor in the treatment of substance misusing adolescents. *Substance Use & Misuse, 31*(8), 1015–1039.

Blumer, H. 1969. *Symbolic interactionism: Perspective and method.* Englewood Cliffs, NJ: Prentice-Hall.

Blumer, H. 1981. Conversation with Thomas J. Morrioni and Harvey A. Farberman. *Symbolic Interaction, 4,* 9–22.

Brown, S. 1985. *Treating the alcoholic: A developmental model of recovery.* New York: John Wiley & Sons.

Brudenell, I. 1997. A grounded theory of protecting recovery during transition to motherhood. *American Journal Drug Alcohol Abuse,* 23(3), 453–466.

Charon, J. 2001. *Symbolic interactionism: An introduction, an interpretation, an integration,* seventh ed. Upper Saddle River, NJ: Prentice Hall.

Chassin, L., C. J. Curran, A. M. Hussong, and C. R. Colder. 1996. The relation of parent alcoholism to adolescent substance use: A longitudinal follow-up study. *Journal of Abnormal Psychology, 105*(1), 70–80.

Clark, H. W., C. L. Masson, K. L. Delucchi, S. M. Hall, and K. L. Sees. 2001. Violent traumatic events and drug abuse severity. *Journal of Substance Abuse Treatment, 20,* 121–127.

Cohen, P. 1987. Cocaine Use in Amsterdam in Non-deviant Subcultures. Paper presented at the International Council on Alcohol and Addictions Congress, Lausanne, Switzerland, June.

Copeland, J. 1998. A qualitative study of self-managed change in substance dependence among women. *Contemporary Drug Problems, 25,* 321–343.

Corbin, J., and A. Strauss. 2008. *Basics of qualitative research,* 3ed. Los Angeles: Sage.

Costa, A. M. (2008). Executive Director, United Nations Office on Drugs and Crime. *World drug report.* New York, NY: United Nations Office on Drugs and Crime.

Costello, R. M. 1975. Alcoholism treatment and evaluation, II: Collation of Two Year Follow-up studies. *International Journal of Addictions,* 10:857–867.

Currie, E. 1993. *Reckoning: Drugs, the cities, and the American future.* New York: Hill and Wang.

Currie, E. (1987). *What kind of future? Violence and public safety in the year 2000.* (Abstract). Rockville, MD: National Institute of Justice. Retrieved January 20, 2010, from http://www.ncjrs.gov/App/Publications/abstract.aspx?ID=107445

Davidson, L., J. Tondora, and M. O'Connell. 2007. Creating a Recovery-Oriented System of Behavioral Health Care: Moving from Concept to Reality. *Psychiatric Rehabilitation Journal, 31*(1), 23–31.

Deci, E. L., and R. M. Ryan. 1985. *Intrinsic motivation and self-determination in human behavior.* New-York: Plenum.

Degenhardt, L., C. Hallam, and D. Bewley-Taylor. (2009). *Comparing the drug situation across countries: Problems, pitfalls and possibilities.* Beckley Foundation Drug Policy Programme, September. Swansea, UK: University of Swansea.

Denzin, N., and Y. Lincoln. 2008. *Collecting and interpreting qualitative materials.* 3rd Ed. Los Angeles: CA: Sage.

Denzin, N. 1987a. *The alcoholic self.* Newbury Park, CA: Sage.

Denzin, N. 1987b. *The recovering alcoholic.* Newbury Park, CA: Sage.

Denzin, N. 1992. *Symbolic interactionism and cultural studies: The politics of interpretation.* Oxford: Blackwell.

DiClemente, C. C., D. Schlundt, and L. Gemmell. 2004. Readiness and stages of change in addiction treatment. *The American Journal on Addictions,* 13:103–119.

Drug Enforcement Administration (DEA). 2009 *Missouri State Factsheet.* US Drug Enforcement Administration. (Accessed July 27, 2010). http://www.dea.gov/pubs/states/missouri.html

Ebaugh, H. R. F. 1988. *Becoming an ex: The process of role-exit.* University of Chicago Press.

Edwards, G. 2000. *Alcohol: The ambiguous molecule.* Toronto, ON: Penguin Books Ltd.

Edwards, G., E. Marshall, and C. Cook. 1997. *The treatment of drinking problems: A guide for the helping professions.* Cambridge University Press.

Elliott, D. S., D. Huizinga, and S. S. Ageton. 1985. *Explaining delinquency and drug use.* Newbury Park, California: Sage Publication Inc.

Ettorre, E. *Women and substance use.* 1992. London: Macmillan.

Fagan, J. A., D. K. Stewart, and K. V. Hansen. 1983. Violent men or violent husbands: Background factors and situational correlates. In D. Finkelhor, R. J. Gelles, G. T. Hotaling, and M. A. Strauss (eds.). *The dark side of families.* Beverly Hills, CA: Sage.

Fergusson, D., J. Boden, and J. Horwood. 2008. Exposure to childhood sexual and physical abuse and adjustment in early adulthood. *Child Abuse & Neglect, 32,* 607–619.

Fiorentine, R., M. L. Pilati, and M. P. Hillhouse. 1999. Drug treatment outcomes: Investigating the long-term effects of sexual and physical abuse histories. *Journal of Psychoactive Drugs, 31*(4), 363–372.

Frykholm, B. 1985. The drug career. *Journal of Drug Issues, 15,* 333–346.

Gatto, C. (2002). *Update: European drug policy: Analysis and case studies.* Washington, DC: The National Organization for the Reform of Marijuana Laws (NORML) Foundation.

Giddens, A. 1984. *The constitution of society.* Cambridge, MA: Polity Press.

Gil-Rivas, V., R. D. Fiorentine, E. Anglin, and E. Taylor. 1997. Sexual and physical abuse: Do they compromise drug treatment outcomes? *Journal of Substance Abuse Treatment, 14*(4), 351–358.

Goffman. E. 1963. *Stigma.* Englewood Cliffs, NJ: Prentice Hall.

Goode, E. 1999. *Drugs in American society.* Fifth ed. Boston: McGraw-Hill.

Gootenberg, P. (2009). Talking about the flow: Drugs, borders, and the discourse of drug control. *Cultural Critique, 71,* (winter). Minneapolis, Minnesota: University of Minnesota Press.

Gordon, D. R. (1994). *Return of the dangerous classes: Drug prohibition and policy politics.* (Abstract). Retrieved January 20, 2010, from http://www.ncjrs.gov/App/Publications/abstract.aspx?ID=158742

Granfield, R., and W. Cloud. 1999. *Coming clean: Overcoming addiction without treatment.* New York: New York University Press.

Grant, B. F., T. C. Harford, D. A Dawson, P. Chou, M. Dufour, and R. Pickering. 1994. Prevalence of DSM-IV alcohol abuse and dependence: United States, 1992. *Alcohol Health and Research World, 18*(3), 243–248.

Grant, J. (2009). A profile of substance abuse, gender, crime, and drug policy in the United States and Canada. *Journal of Offender/Rehabilitation, 48,* 1–15.

Grella, C. E., and V. Joshi. 1999. Gender difference in drug treatment careers among clients in the national drug abuse treatment outcome study. *The American Journal of Drug and Alcohol Abuse, 25*(3), 385–406.

Haas, J. 2003. *Seeking bliss: The study of addiction and recovery.* Victoria, British Columbia: Mosaic.

Haight, W., T. Jacobsen, J. Black, L. Kingery, K. Sheridan, and C. Mulder. 2005.'In These Days': Parent Methamphetamine Abuse and Child Welfare in the Rural Midwest. *Children and Youth Services Review, 27,* 949–971.

Hallam, C., and D. Bewley-Taylor. (2010). Mapping the world drug problem: Science and politics in the United Nations drug control system (Editorial). *International Journal of Drug Policy, 21,* 1–3.

Haseltine, F. 2000. Gender differences in addiction and recovery. *Journal of Women's Health and Gender-Based Medicine, 9*(6), 579–583.

Havassy, B. E., S. M. Hall, and D. A. Wasserman. 1991. Social support and relapse: Commonalities among alcoholics, opiate users, and cigarette smokers. *Addictive Behaviors, 16,* 235–246.

Heirich, M. 1977. Change of heart: A test of some widely held theories about religious conversion. *American Journal of Sociology, 83,* 653–680.

Herz, D. C. 2000. *Drugs in the heartland: Methamphetamine use in rural Nebraska.* Washington, DC: National Institute of Justice.

Hser, Y., D. Huang, C. Teruya, and A. Anglin. 2003. Gender comparisons of drug abuse treatment outcomes and predictors. *Drug and Alcohol Dependence, 72,* 255–264.

Hughes, J. A. 1976. *Sociological analysis: Methods of discovery.* London: Nelson.

Irwin, T., and J. Morgenstern. 2005. Drug-use patterns among men who have sex with men presenting for alcohol treatment: Differences in ethnic and sexual identity. *Journal of Urban Health: Bulletin of the New York Academy of Medicine, 82*(1), 127–133.

Jacobs, D. 1989. *A general theory of addictions: Rationale for and evidence supporting a new approach for understanding and treating addictive behaviors.* Lexington, MA: Lexington Books.

Jellinek, E. M. 1952. Phases of alcohol addiction. *Quarterly Journal of Studies on Alcohol, 7,* 673–684.

Johnson, S., J. Listwan, A. Sundt, M. Holsinger, and E. Latessa. 2003. The Effect of Drug Court Programming on Recidivism: The Cincinnati Experience. *Crime and Delinquency, 49*(3), 389–411.

Josselson, R. 1996. *Revising herself: The story of women's identity from college to midlife.* San Francisco: Jossey-Bass.

Kandel, D., and V. H. Raveis. 1989. Cessation of drug use in young adulthood. *Archives of General Psychiatry, 46,* 109–116.

Karp, C. L., T. L. Butler, and S. C. Bergsdtram. 1998. *Treatment strategies for abused adolescents from victim to survivor.* Thousand Oaks, CA: Sage Publications.

Keys, D. P., and J. F. Galliher. 2000. *Confronting the drug control establishment: Alfred Lindesmith as a public intellectual.* Albany, New York: State University of New York Press.

Kiecolt, K. 1994. Stress and the decision to change oneself: A theoretical model. *Social Psychological Quarterly,* 57, 49–63.

Klingemann, H. 1991. The motivation for change from problem alcohol and heroin use. *British Journal of the Addictions, 86,* 727–744.

Klingemann, H. 1992. Coping and maintenance strategies of spontaneous remitters from problem use of alcohol and heroin in Switzerland. *The International Journal of the Addictions, 27*(12), 1359–1388.

Leonard, K. E., and H. T. Blane. 1992. Alcohol and marital aggression in a national sample of young men. *Journal of Interpersonal Violence,* 7(1), 19–30.

Leonard, K. E., E. J. Bromet, D. K. Parkinson, N. L. Day, and C. M. Ryan. 1985. Patterns of alcohol use and physically aggressive behavior in men. *Journal of Studies on Alcohol, 46,* 279–282.

Liebschutz, J., J. B. Savetsky, R. Saitz, N. J. Horton, C. Lloyd-Travaglini, and J. H. Samet. 2002. The relationship between sexual and physical abuse and substance abuse consequences. *Journal of Substance Abuse Treatment, 22,* 121–128.

Lindesmith, A. 1968. *Addiction and opiates.* Chicago: Aldine.

Litman, G. K., J. Stapleton, A. N. Oppenheim, M. Peleg, and P. Jackson. 1983. Situations related to alcoholism relapse. *British Journal of Addiction,* 78:381–389.

Lofland, J. 1966. *Doomsday cult: A study of conversion, proselytization, and maintenance of faith.* Englewood Cliffs, New Jersey: Prentice-Hall, Inc.

Lofland, J., and R. Stark. 1965. Becoming a world-saver: A theory of conversion to a deviant perspective. *American Sociological Review, 30,* 862–75.

MacPherson, D. 2001. *A framework for action: A four-pillar approach to drug problems in Vancouver.* Vancouver, BC: City of Vancouver.

Majer, J. M., L. A. Jason, J. R. Ferrari, and C. S. North. 2002.Comorbidity among Oxford house residents: A preliminary outcome study. *Addictive Behaviors, 27,* 837–845.

Marlatt, G. A., J. S. Baer, D. M. Donovan, and D. R. Kivlahan. 1988. Addictive behaviors: Etiology and treatment. *Annual Review Psychology, 39,* 223–252.

Maruna, S. 2001. *Making good: How ex-convicts reform and rebuild their lives.* Washington, DC: American Psychological Association.

Mauer, M., and R. King. 2007. *A 25-year quagmire: The war on drugs and its impact on American society.* Washington, DC: The Sentencing Project.

McIntosh, J., and N. McKeganey. 2002. *Beating the dragon: The recovery from dependent drug use.* Harlow, England: Prentice-Hall.

McMahon, M. 1995. *Engendering motherhood: Identity and self-transformation in women's lives.* New York: Guilford.

McMurran, M. 1994. *The psychology of addiction.* London: Taylor & Francis.

Mead, G. H. 1934. *Mind, self and society from the standpoint of a social behaviorist.* Edited by C. Morris. Chicago: University of Chicago Press.

Mead, G. H. 1938. *The philosophy of the act.* Chicago: University of Chicago Press.

Miller, W. R. 1998. Why do people change addictive behavior? The 1996 H. David Archibald lecture. *Addiction, 93*(2), 163–172.

Miller, W. R., and V. C. Sanchez. 1994. Motivating young adults for treatment and lifestyle change. In G. S. Nathan & P. E. Nathan (Eds.), *Alcohol use and misuse by young adults* (pp. 55–81). Notre Dame, IN: University of Notre Dame Press.

Missouri Department of Mental Health, Division of Alcohol and Drug Abuse (April 2008). Status Report on Missouri's Alcohol and Drug Abuse Problems.

Moen, T. 2006. Reflections on the narrative research approach. *International Journal of Qualitative Methods, 5*(4).

Murphy, S., and M. Rosenbaum. 1999. *Pregnant women on drugs: Combating stereotypes and stigma.* New Brunswick, NJ: Rutgers University Press.

Neale, J., S. Nettleton, and L. Pickering. 2011. Recovery from problem drug use: What can we learn from the sociologist Erving Goffman? *Drugs: education, prevention and policy, 18*(1), 3–9.

Neale, J., D. Allen, and L. Coombes. 2005. Qualitative research methods within the addictions. *Addiction,* pp. 1584–1593.

Nurco, D. N., T. W. Kinlock, K. E. O'Grady, and T. E. Hanlon. 1998. Differential contributions of family and peer factors to the etiology of narcotic addiction. *Drug and Alcohol Dependence, 51,* 229–237.

Olenick, N. L., and D. Chalmers. 1991. Gender-specific drinking styles in alcoholics and nonalcoholics. *Journal of Studies on Alcohol, 52*(4), 325–330.

Peele, S. 1989. *The diseasing of America: Addiction treatment out of control.* Lexington, MA: Lexington Books.

Peters, R. H., A. L. Strozier, M. R. Murrin, and W. D. Kearns. 1997. Treatment of substance-abusing jail inmates: Examination of gender differences. *Journal of Substance Abuse Treatment, 14,* 339–349.

Pirard, S., E. Sharon, S. K. Kang, G. A. Angarita, and D. R. Gastfriend. 2005. Prevalence of physical and sexual abuse among substance abuse patients and impact on treatment outcomes. *Drug and Alcohol Dependence, 78,* 57–64.

Powis, B., P. Griffiths, M. Gossop, and J. Strang. 1996. The difference between male and female drug users: Community samples of heroin and cocaine users compared. *Substance Use and Misuse, 31*(5), 529–543.

Prince, G. (2000[1990]). On Narratology (Past, Present, Future). In M. McQuillan (ed.) *The narrative reader,* p. 129. London: Routledge.

Prochaska, J., J. Norcross, and C. DiClemente. 1994. *Changing for good: A revolutionary six-change program for overcoming bad habits and moving your life positively forward.* New York: Avon.

Prochaska, J. O., C. C. DiClemente, and J. C. Norcross. 1992. In search of how people change. Applications to addictive behaviors. *American Psychologist, 47*(9), 1102–1114.

Reiger D. A., M. E. Farmer, D. S. Rae, B. Z. Locke, S. J. Keith, L. L. Judd, and F. K. Goodwin. 1990. Comorbidity of mental disorders with alcohol and other drug abuse. Results from the Epidemiologic Catchment Area (ECA) Study. *Journal of American Medical Association, 264,* (19), 2511–2518.

Riley, D. (1998). *Drugs and drug policy in Canada: A brief review & commentary.* Canadian Foundation for Drug Policy & International Harm Reduction Association. Ottawa, ON: Canada.

Rosenbaum, M. 1981. *Women on heroin.* New Brunswick, NJ: Rutgers University Press.

Rudy, D. 1986. *Becoming alcoholic: Alcoholics Anonymous and the reality of alcoholism.* Carbondale: Southern Illinois University Press.

Sandstrom, K., D. Martin, and G. Fine. 2003. *Symbols, selves, and social reality: A symbolic interactionist approach to social psychology and sociology.* Los Angeles: Roxbury.

Schober, R., and H. Annis. 1996. Barriers to help-seeking for change in drinking: A gender-focused review of the literature. *Addictive Behaviors, 21*(1), 81–92.

Schwarzer, R. 2001. Social-cognitive factors in changing health-related behavior. *Current Directions in Psychological Science, 10*(2), 47–51.

Shaffer, H. 1996. Understanding the means and objects of addiction: Technology, the internet and gambling. *Journal of Gambling Studies*, Vol. 12(4), 461–469.

Shaffer, H. J., and S. B. Jones. 1989. *Quitting cocaine: The struggle against impulse.* Lexington, MA: Lexington Books.

Shank, G. (2002). *Qualitative research. A personal skills approach.* New Jersey: Prentice Hall.

Singer, J. (2004). Narrative identity and meaning making across the adult lifespan: An introduction. *Journal of Personality, 72*(3), 437–59.

Simoneau, H., and J. Bergeron. 2003. Factors affecting motivation during the first six weeks of treatment. *Addictive Behaviors, 28*, 1219–1241.

Simpson, D. D., G. W. Joe, W. E. K. Lehman, and S. B. Sells. 1986. Addiction careers: Etiology, treatment and 12 year follow up outcomes. *Journal of Drug Issues, 16*(1), 107–121.

Smart, R. G. 1994. Dependence and correlates of change: A review of the literature. In G. Edwards and M. Lader (Eds.), *Addiction: Processes of change.* Oxford, England: Oxford University Press.

Smith, C. 1991. Healing the feminine: A feminist residential model for treating chemical dependency. In Van Den Berg, Nan (Ed.). *Feminist perspectives on addiction.* New York: Springer Publishing.

Snow, D. M. 1997. How recovering addicted women succeed. *Journal of Addictions Nursing, 9*(4), 182–189.

Sobell, L. C., J. A. Cunningham, and M. B. Sobell. 1996. Natural recovery is the predominant pathway to recovery from alcohol problems: Results from two general population surveys. *American Journal of Public Health, 86*(7), 966–972.

Sobell, L. C., M. B. Sobell, T. Toneatto, and G. I. Leo. 1993. What triggers the resolution of alcohol problems without treatment? *Alcoholism: Clinical and experimental research*, 17, 217–224.

Springer, J., J. Sheridan, D. Kuo, and M. Carnes. 2007. Long-term physical and mental health consequences of childhood physical abuse: Results from a large population based sample of men and women. *Child Abuse and Neglect, 31*(5), 517–530. doi:10.1016/j.chiabu.2007.01.003.

Stanley, L., and B. Temple. 2008. Narrative methodologies: Subjects, silences, re-readings and analyses. *Qualitative Research, 8*(3), 275–281.

Stephens, R. 1991. *The street addict role: A theory of heroin addiction.* Albany: State University of New York Press.

Stevens, A., D. Berto, U. Frick, T. McSweeney, S. Schaaf, M. Tartari, P. Turnbull, B. Trinkl, A. Uchtenhagen, G. Waidner, and W. Werdenich. 2007. The victimization of dependent drug users: Findings from a European study. *European Society of Criminology,* 4(4), 385–408, 1477–3708.

Stone, G. 1962. Appearance and the self. In Arnold Rose, ed., *Human behavior and social processes,* 86–118. Boston: Houghton Mifflin.

Straus, R. A. 1976. Changing oneself: Seekers and the creative transformation of life experience. In J. Lofland (ed.). *Doing social life: The qualitative study of human interaction.* New York: Wiley.

Substance Abuse and Mental Health Services Administration (SAMHSA), Office of Applied Studies, National Survey on Drug Use and Health, 2004, 2005, 2006, and 2007.

Sussman, S.; S. Skara, and S. Ames. 2008. Substance abuse among adolescents. *Substance Use & Misuse,* 43:1802–1828.

Taber, J. 1993. *Addictive behavior: An informal clinical view.* Reno: Nevada: University of Nevada.

Terry, C. 2003. *The fellas: Overcoming prison and addiction.* Belmont, CA: Wadsworth Thomson Learning.

Tims, F. and C. Leukefeld. 1986. *Relapse and recovery in drug abuse.* NIDA Research Monograph 72. Department of Health and Human Services. Rockville, Maryland. Alcohol, Drug Abuse, and Mental Health Administration. National Institute on Drug Abuse.

Travisano, R. 1970. Alternation and conversion as qualitatively different transformations. In Gregory Stone and Harvey Farberman (Eds.). *Social psychology through symbolic interaction.* New York: John Wiley.

Turner, R. 1978. The role and the person. *American Journal of Sociology,* 84(1), 1–21.

Underhill, B. 1991. Recovery needs of lesbian alcoholics in treatment. In Nan Van Den Bergh (ed.). *Feminist perspectives on addiction.* New York: Springer Publishing Co.

Vaillant, G. E. 1983. Natural history of male alcoholism: Is alcoholism the cart or the horse to sociopathy? *British Journal of Addiction,* 78, 317–326.

Vaillant, G. E. 1995. *The natural history of alcoholism revisited.* Cambridge, MA: Harvard University Press.

Van Den Bergh, N. 1991. Having bitten the apple: A feminist perspective on addictions. In *Feminist perspectives on addiction,* Nan Van Den Bergh (ed.). 3–30. New York: Springer.

Vygotsky, L. S. 1978. Mind in society: The development of higher psychological processes. Cambridge, MA: Harvard University Press.

Waldorf, D. 1983. Natural recovery from opiate addiction: Some social-psychological processes of untreated recovery. *Journal of Drug Issues,* 237–280.

Waldorf, D., and P. Biernacki. 1981. The natural recovery from opiate addiction: Some preliminary findings. *Journal of Drug Issues,* 11(1), 61–74.

Waldorf, D., C. Reinarman, and S. Murphy. 1991. *Cocaine changes: The experience of using and quitting.* Philadelphia: Temple University Press.

Walker, R. (Ed.). 1985. *Applied qualitative research.* Aldershot, UK: Gower.

Weigert, A. J., S. Tiege, and D. Tiege. 1986. *Society and identity.* New York: Cambridge University Press.

Whiteacre, K. n.d. The cultural milieu of criminology and drug research. Ph.D. Student, Indiana University Department of Criminal Justice. Retrieved September 20, 2010, from http://www.drugpolicy.org/docUploads/milieu.pdf

White, W. 2007. Addiction recovery: Its definition and conceptual boundaries. *Journal of Substance Abuse Treatment,* 33, 229–241.

Winick, C. 1962. Maturing out of narcotic addiction. *UN Bulletin on Narcotics,* *41*(1), 1–7.

Young, J. (n.d.). *Critical criminology in the 21st century: Critique, irony and the always unfinished.* Retrieved September 20, 2010, from Http://www.malcolmread.co.uk/jockyoung/Critical.htm

Youth Online Comprehensive Results. 2008. Centers for Disease Control and Prevention, Atlanta, GA.

Zuber-Skerritt, O. 2001. Action learning and action research: Paradigm, praxis and programs. In S. Sankaran, B. Dick, R. Passfield, and P. Swepson (Eds.), *Effective change management using action learning and action research: Concepts, frameworks, processes, applications,* 1–20. Lismore: Southern Cross University.

Zurcher, L. 1977. *The mutable self.* Beverly Hills, CA: Sage.

Index

175

About the Book

Judith Grant explores the experiences of men who grapple with drug and alcohol abuse, illuminating the interplay between individual identity and social environment that shapes the processes of addiction and recovery.

Grant draws on the voices of the men themselves as she traces and analyzes their paths to both addiction and desistance. Documenting the full sweep of their journeys, she also highlights the critical differences and similarities in the experiences of men and women.

Judith Grant is assistant professor of criminology, justice, and policy at University of Ontario Institute of Technology.